One Day, One Night at a Time

WOMEN WRITE OF POVERTY, HOMELESSNESS, AND HOPE

Members of
The Gathering Place

Printed in the United States of America, by Lightning Source, Inc.

ISBN 978-1-937862-38-1
Library of Congress Control Number 2013904597

Published 2013 by BookCrafters, Parker, Colorado.
SAN-859-6352, BookCrafters@comcast.net
http://self-publish-your-book.com

Title *One Day, One Night at a Time* taken from "The Whisper of the Wind" by Peg Butler
Artwork in *One Day, One Night at a Time* is by women in the Writers' Group

Cover art by Sharon Kumm

Copies of this book may be ordered from www.bookcrafters.net and www.tgpdenver.org

BookCrafters

Dedication

*To all who share the experiences of homelessness and poverty
and to those who may still be searching for their voice.*

Introduction

For people who are experiencing homelessness and poverty, there are few opportunities for creative expression. Creativity is relegated to the place of luxury – only accessed after the work has been done. And for this group of people, the work is seldom done. Living in poverty is in and of itself, hard work. Housing and food need to be secured; medical and mental health care accessed. School, employment or some kind of regular income must be obtained, and transportation to appointments coordinated. Understanding and meeting the requirements of a complicated and often disjointed system is exhausting. In 1986, The Gathering Place was founded as a safe place where women and children would receive assistance in this hard work and where they might find community and hope as they navigated life's challenges.

Our members, or those we serve, come from a wide variety of backgrounds. Their education level ranges from hardly any to those with advanced degrees. They live on the street, in shelters, and in their own homes. They represent all races and ethnicities, come from stable homes and the borrowed homes of foster care. Many are victims of family violence; some have mental illness; some have been incarcerated. Yet we share a common humanity that brings us together as we identify our strengths and struggles and our hopes and dreams.

Each day our members choose from an array of possibilities designed to offer choice and promote positive relationships. Three meals a day and "the coffee pot on" create opportunities for informal friendships, as well as access to nutrition. Mothers with children work together on finding resources for themselves and their families. Those seeking education use computers and attend classes that support adult learning. Collaborations with other organizations result in easier access to medical care, mental health care, and housing. Hundreds of volunteers ensure that our members are surrounded by people from the community who want to connect with others and be a part of the solution to homelessness. Haircuts, showers, and clothing help renew self-worth. The Thursday Writers' Group is one of our many programs and is the source of the writings in this book.

The Gathering Place has always valued self-expression and over the years we have learned that stories can be told in many voices. Writing, visual art, fiber arts, and various music programs have all provided forums for storytelling and for moving out of the shadows and into the light. Art, in all its forms, allows us to find meaning in our experiences. Sharing our art can give others a glimpse into what we value and how we feel.

As the world has evolved to one where we value a sense of life balance, we still seem to have an expectation that people who are living in poverty should be constantly working earnestly on getting out and achieving the great dream of economic stability. For women, children, and people who are transgendered, The Gathering Place has been a refuge where that dream has not been separated from the context of individual lives. Recognizing that each person has a history and a story that has led to her current situation, it has always been our goal to listen and learn and to honor the story and the storytelling. By encouraging creativity in writing and other art forms, our members can tap into new or lost strengths and find both the skills and the energy necessary to face each day, "One Day, One Night at a Time."

Leslie R. Foster
President & CEO
The Gathering Place

Preface

The Gathering Place opens its arms to women in many wonderful ways, but one small class defies easy description, for this is where members often find pathways directly to their truth.

Some rush in, bursting with words that start to pour out as soon as pen hits paper; others can't find an easy track from head to hand so stay in quiet reflection until the secrets of their hearts begin to seep out. A few just sit and think, free for a while from the spin of a world gone awry. All visibly relax as they enter an emotional zone where anything is possible. They have arrived in Writers' Group, where armor cracks and healing begins.

A class that arose from a wish became a book that evolved from a dream, a desire that healing words venture beyond a classroom to journey into the world. For seven years, this group of ever-changing participants has met weekly to tell tales and seek pathways, generating over a thousand poems, stories, letters, and essays along the way. We who serve as facilitators offer encouragement, gentle guidance, and positive feedback, knowing these pieces are not intended to be exercises in literary perfection but to speak the language of the heart. Tears fall, hugs happen, and a cleansing emerges as the women come to understand that their experiences are singular but not unique to them.

Although often reticent at first, the writers soon find their own voices, deciding which parts of their lives to reveal and examining feelings as they spill onto paper. They learn to trust both their instincts and each other by writing and sharing hidden parts of their lives. Long-buried secrets shrink in the light, losing their fraudulent power; courage and hope replace anger and humiliation. Inspired by the truth of others, writers come to believe that their own struggles can be surmounted and that their voices are powerful and valid.

Some write only a few sentences, others dash off pages. Poetry, the art whose complexity defies containment, has emerged as the genre of primary choice for many, because it's less complex to craft in simple form yet has the ability to speak profoundly with a few carefully-chosen words. Since most writers don't have computer access, we type each piece and return it so they can see their words transfer from a written scrawl to a legitimate piece of literature. An important part of our process is to give the women assistance with their writing skills along the way, but the final decisions on content and language are always theirs; therefore, the pieces submitted were ultimately edited only for spelling and punctuation.

The collected writings of women who live on the edge of society's systems—in shelters, on the streets, in warrens of subsidized apartments—bring a simple eloquence to complex histories. We invite you to move beyond your comfort zone as you read the raw and arduous stories contained within these pages. Be also prepared to have a heart-opening, spirit-lifting experience as you enter a world that may exist far beyond your knowing. These women are survivors—determined, courageous, and eternally hopeful as they work to once again find solid ground. May their honest words allow you to see the world through other eyes and bring visibility to invisible lives.

Kirsten Morgan and Suzanne Burm

Acknowledgments

The essence of The Gathering Place is our sense of community and connectedness. We impact each other in all ways and hence, our greatest accomplishments are shared. Indeed, this book would not have happened without the profound support of many.

Our thanks to the Board of Directors who didn't even flinch when we proposed in our annual business plan that this year we "write a book." Their belief in and support of our organization makes all things possible.

Thanks to The Gathering Place staff who encourage people to attend the Writers' Group and provide the resources and support that allow our members to recognize their strengths. We are so proud that some of the writing within acknowledges this kindness.

Our heartfelt thanks to all of our volunteers who make The Gathering Place a safe place to be and to take risks; where countless people are available because they want to be, not because they are paid to be. Kirsten and Suzanne stand high among them. Thank you both for believing in the writers and for your patience and guidance throughout this remarkable journey.

Thanks to our editors and publishers, Joe and Jan, who gave us hope, a vision, and the technical experience we needed to realize our dream.

Finally, and most importantly, thank you to the members of The Gathering Place with whom we share our lives, our stories, and our inspiration.

Quiet
Leticia D. Tanguma

Away from "fitting in."
Away from "majority rule."
Away from annoying or threatening traffic.

Away to breathe.
To co-exist with kindred spirits,
To laugh, write, share, listen.

I made it to Writers' Group
With a sigh of relief
This Thursday afternoon.

Here I want to live.

Here I dream of the future.

Here I have hope.

Courage
BJ

I meet many courageous people every day. What one sees as hardship, another sees as opportunity. We have an opportunity to make choices every day—but will I remember 10 years from now which of my choices got me there? Do I remember 10 years? Only in little chunks.

Time can be boxed—boxes are to open, one at a time. When I don't like what's in my box, I put it back in. I think I need more courage to take it out of the box and turn it around so I can really see it. Why are boxes such a big deal to my family—my kids and grandkids? Because they can hold anything, or maybe because they are so versatile.

Surprises can come in boxes—the best surprise I ever gave was two large, wrapped and ribboned boxes to my kids at Christmas when I thought I had nothing to give. But the empty boxes held dreams that poured out in abundance as my kids played with them year after year.

How odd. Sometimes I am scared to open my own boxes, but I don't mind giving empty ones to my kids—odd—funny-odd—and that gives me courage to open my own because, I remind myself, if only I will really look, I can turn my things over and see them from a different perspective, and suddenly they don't have the same hold on me.

My Experience With Crying
Essie Mae Thomas

One night I sat crying and crying.
It started with just my thinking,
going back in my past. So, then I began
crying and crying. There's really nothing
wrong with crying. I don't care

who you are, where you've been,
rich or poor, even the color of your skin;
all of our blood is red. Doesn't matter
how much money you've lost. Perhaps
you've lost a loved one—husband, wife,
child, niece, nephew, even your best friend.

We all have lost something.
But whatever the reason for your crying,
it's cleansing. You may have held something in
or even held a grudge. You held that thing
in so long until now you are crying.
So what I say to you today is
it's OK for your crying.

Two Women
eb

They sit in a corner,
squatting figures
on a floor

in a room full of women.

If you didn't know them,
you wouldn't notice

how happy and content

they seemed,

faces aglow, smiling,
catching up on the latest.

To anyone else,
these women might seem
insignificant,
but they are happy
because
they have made it.

Small hurdles.
They are reunited after a time
apart.

Last time they saw each other
was a cold, harsh day

when both were helpless and
uncertain of what the next day
would bring.
Neither knew what the next step
would be.

That was six months ago.

Today, things look different for them.
Last time one woman was bound
by an abusive relationship,
the other had only her car
to live in.

Now. Today
they smile.

To anyone else,
this is elementary.

These are small steps,
but today is special.

Today spells freedom.

It is special because they share
a common bond,
a holy fire; they have jumped
a hurdle.

This is a women's homeless shelter.
They see the hordes of women
come into the place,

holding everything they own,
some looking bewildered.

they know the feeling;
they have been there.

But today is truly special,

because today,
they are blessed;

they have each other.

Magic Soup
Paula Cordier

Five children are stranded in a cabin deep in the wilderness, while snow builds up outside, almost reaching the tops of the windows. Darkness has fallen and the howls of starving wolves echo and reverberate through the too-thin walls as they circle around, looking for a way in.

Supplies are running low. The oldest child, a girl, sighs heavily as she looks through barren cupboards and finally opens the fridge. Eggs, but no milk. The younger ones are hungry.

They ate the last two cans of Spaghettios earlier, the big sister carefully spooning even amounts into every bowl but hers. She can go without a few spoons when it comes to her beloved siblings.

The youngest two, boys, look up at her with worried eyes. "It's okay," she reassures them. "I saved the best meal for last. A wizard gave me the recipe, so it's magic!"

The big sister starts the water boiling on the stove while her brothers look on. After adding the secret ingredients and saying some magic words, she cracks the eggs into the pot one by one as she stirs carefully, letting her brothers take a turn.

After sitting them down at the table and serving up their magic soup, her two little brothers look down at it dubiously. The other two girls don't say a word as they slurp theirs down. After more coaxing, the boys give in too, their growling tummies and child's belief in magic giving way.

A single space heater heats up the living room where they'll bed down for the night. Blankets are laid down in the middle of the floor, where the five kids will lie helter skelter, curling up into one another for warmth, with more blankets piled on top.

The wind whistles through loose windowpanes and doorjambs, giving them all a fright. The oldest girl starts weaving adventurous tales for them all to get lost in, her soothing voice making them feel safe and secure as they snuggle closer.

The oldest child is fiercely protective of them. They belong to her. She's the one who wipes their tears and kisses them better, the one who tells them stories, and makes up games for them to play. She's the one they look up to for protection. She's their big sister, after all.

A key in the lock as the doorknob turns. Their real mother is back. Everything the big sister has done unravels in seconds as her brothers and sisters jump up excitedly. "Mama, Mama," they all cry out. The oldest child stands back, the betrayal of their joy piercing her heart.

The world swims into clearer focus. The house is unkempt, with clothes and toys scattered about haphazardly. The snow outside is gone, the sound of the wolves replaced by the sound of cars driving past their house.

The happy reunion takes away the adventure magic until next time their mother leaves them all alone. For hours or days—the girl is too young to know the concept of time. The oldest sister knows only that she lives for those times when she is her sisters' and brothers' everything. When they belong to her, and her alone.

Light Upon the Lightness
Sharon Kumm

I wanted to light upon the lightness,
the unseen, by writing. Hear me
calling—the depth that I've seen and
sunk into, heard and shimmied up to.
Is that why they call it understanding,
because it comes from below?

I kissed his meaning, but I wanted more
of a touch beneath my feet—in the grass
of the unmanifest, where my eyes saw, and
my ears too, the atoms moving slowly.

Widen my grasp, narrow my fear of being
absolutely alone here. My home no longer
mine—trails of lives here, disappearing
in the dusk. Is there dust
when the sun goes down?

In my turning, when I felt the butterfly
opening of peace and beauty,
what was it—I still felt unfinished—
but the signs were there, the growing
being in the mirror, the parts of me—
my mind and body recognizing
a desire for homelessness.

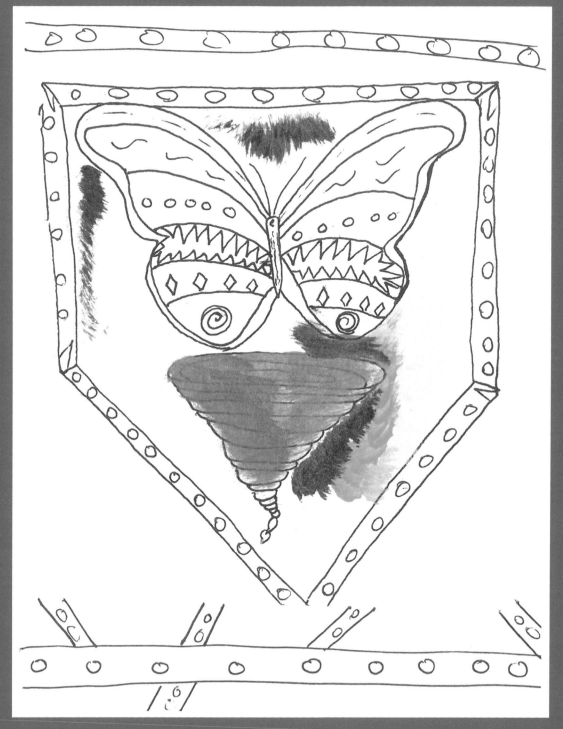

Micole L. Lane

The Babies Were Happy to Leave
BJ

Grease-smudged, smiling faces,
Water at a premium
Grubby hands reach out,
Waiting for the world to fall into them.
Bright eyes flash under smoke-infused hair,
Taking in new sights
While noses tingle with new smells.

Stern eyes fall upon them, empty eyes
Filling with disgust before
Swilling full of pointed anger.
"Heathens! Unclean! Like wild animals!"
The words slam against baby ears
Not yet able to understand their meaning.
Smiles waver, eyes dim, noses sense danger.

Spirits recoil from the icy blast of contempt.
Pristine white sheets, clean towels,
New clothes shoved into tiny arms,
Becoming a heavy burden to babies
Marked forever with ugly memories
That will be theirs for a lifetime,
While tiny hearts quietly cry for Mama.

Tunkasila, who were these people
Who taught us to hate,
To hate ourselves and each other
At such a tender age?
To hate, so we can be clean and white
And civilized, just like them.
The babies were so happy when they left…

I am here to reclaim them.
I come with tenderness and love
To wrap them in my arms,
Filling them with comfort and peace,
To return their memories to them
Of lifetimes past, with their strong
Lakota mothers, their families, their Tiyospayes.

Tunkasila, bless all the babies
So their hearts will heal,
So they can smile again, knowing
They come from a fierce
And noble people, a red-skinned people,
A proud people, knocked down only for a time.
The babies will be happy to come home.

To Feel Like I'm a Person
Kim Holder

Thought after thought—
speed thinking and speed walking.
From Greyhound to Sinclair
to public toilets, churches, shelters,
Starbucks, restaurants.
Paper towels off the floor,
flushing and cleaning the sink,
making the trash compact.

Serving.

Cleaning hundreds of bathrooms.
Homeless for five years,
cleaning the toilet was something
I'd do if I had a home.
.
Every single bathroom I entered
was a sparkling palace
when I left it. I wanted productivity
and cleanliness; I wanted to serve
others and I needed to have something
to do that was like housekeeping,
like having a home.

Serving others,
and feeling like
a person.

Black Box
Leticia D. Tanguma

My words are unspoken
but alive in a dance from yesterday,
hopping in a black box theatre,
swirling on a painted floor,
resonating with rhythm and beat.

Words that waited for dance
too long in a little apartment,
in a broken down car or
on a crowded bus, smelling
like urine, cigarette smoke and dust,
or in line at the food bank.

But yesterday morning the words
came alive through dance and
exploring unlimited possibilities,
breaking presumptions of age and ability
with ironic twist and inspirational turns
within the black box.

Sharon Kumm

Freezing

Jennie K. Foster

I saw a lady
by the road
in a wheelchair,
freezing.

I went home
and got her a coat.

I felt pain
that she sat there,
needing something.
She didn't hold a sign;
she just sat there,
freezing.

Lost
C.M. Davidson-Sole

I've lost money, cars, oh my stars,
I've lost my place to live;

lost freedom, time, I've lost my mind,
my faith, my hope, my gifts.

I've lost my shape, I've lost my teeth;
I put them on the shelf.

Vision, hearing, friends disappearing,
my job, oh yeah, my wealth.

Days, weeks, months and years, I think
I lost my stride. No privacy or dignity;
the inner me has died.

I've lost my goal, my roll, my soul
and my emotions too. My health,
my tears, but not my fears.
I think they've multiplied.

Happiness, peace and harmony, oh gee!
My life's a mess. I've lost my temper,
balance and youth, plus
all my interests.

I've lost some toys and some boys,
I've lost some interviews. Some men,
my pen, my socks, my thoughts, and yes,
my point of view.

Lost my glasses and some classes,
and some poems too. Lost my insight
and an invite, lost a couple of screws.

Although I've lost a lot of stuff, I'll
keep on plodding and fight
the good fight here on earth
until my days are through.

How to Come Up With the Rent Money
Elizabeth Vonaarons

It's Monday, June 13th. I have managed to pay $295 of my monthly rent payment, which is $635. This leaves a balance due of $340, which was actually due on June 5th. Last month, May, 2011, the Senior Resource Center helped me pay half of my rent, but that was only a one-time occasion. What to do?

I check with The Gathering Place. They say they will help me with rent for the new place that I had applied to and was accepted. However, I will not be able to move in until August. Since I am not homeless, she cannot help me with my June rent.

So, I get out the handy resource list and call. First, I call Access Housing, between 8:30 and 9:00 a.m., Monday through Thursday. The phone message says they have funds available and someone will call me back. The second day, I hear from Access Housing. They have federal monies for rental assistance and one of the requirements is to take a twelve-week course about finding jobs.

"Can you do that?" the woman on the phone asks.

"Well, OK, yes I can," I say.

I then go over to DenUM (Denver Urban Ministries). They do not have any funds available, but St. Paul Lutheran Church may have funds. Go there between 2:00 and 4:00 because there is a lottery drawing. I go to St. Paul's and get there at 1:45. People are waiting for the doors to open. There is a family there with two small children. The doors open right at 2:00.

I draw lottery number 17 and the lady sitting at my table draws number 14. Since they start with number 1, we are probably not going to be seen by anyone that day. That turns out to be the case but the good news is they have a very nice lunch set up for us. We thank them for the nice lunch.

At 4:00, they announce that this is it for Tuesday but we are welcome to come back for the drawing again on Thursday afternoon. It turns out that Cindy, the lady sitting at my table, is diabetic. Cindy went to the church to ask for monies for her prescriptions. She had to make a decision between filling her prescriptions and getting food. Her food stamp program was in the process of renewing, so she was without food stamps. Food won over prescriptions, so Cindy had been without medication for two months.

I tell her that I will help her out with getting some food. All of her efforts had not been in vain. Then, I get a bright idea.

"How old are you, Cindy?"

"I'm 55," she said.

"Senior Resource Center can probably help you and they are only six blocks away. Maybe we can both get some bus tokens."

We trudge over to the Senior Resource Center. The person for Cindy to talk to about prescriptions is not there, so she makes an appointment for the next morning. They do give us bus tokens though.

We get on the bus and head for King Soopers. Fresh cod is on sale. Cindy gets the things she needs and I tell her that we need to get some fish, two pounds each. We do. I pay for the groceries and we go on our separate ways. Although I still have the June rent problem, this is a very good day for me.

In this whole rent saga, I have not heard from my landlord about why the rent is late or when will I get the balance paid. This is a little scary because silence is equated with fear of the unknown.

On Thursday, I receive a letter and a thank you card in the mail from my sister in northern Wisconsin. I had sent her fudge, which she received the day after she sent her letter. The letter includes a check for $200. I also have another check for $30 from a client I did some gardening for.

That still leaves me $110 left to pay for June rent. Now, what about Cindy?

I call Cindy. She did go to the Senior Resource Center the next day. They did not have a program to help her with prescriptions but they did pay her utilities for her, which she had been behind on for months. They also set her up with a social worker at West Side Clinic to help her with her much-needed prescriptions. A round of applause to the Senior Resource Center!

On Monday it rains. No gardening for me. On Tuesday and Wednesday I garden. Still short on the rent, I decide to ask two other people for help. Worst case scenario is that I will get some gardening monies at the end of the week.

The next day I say to myself, "Bag it with asking for monies for rent." I garden instead. Gardening gives me a sense of accomplishment. The results are almost immediate and I am physically tired. I also believe in the laws of the Universe. The rent situation will be alleviated and we'll all live happily ever after!

The Old Watering Hole
Eleanor L. Josey

Reminds me of the "ole watering hole"
near the village where the women of the village

come to wash clothes, bathe, prepare meals
and discuss the latest events in the village.

The children play safely, nearby,
while the women go about their tasks.

Pretty much, the women and children
get their needs met in this safe place.

They network, trade, prepare, learn, pray
and gather at The Gathering Place.

I thank God for this ole watering hole!

Homelessness
Kathy Lakes

There is homelessness
everywhere. Everyone
needs a helping hand now
and then. They need
encouragement and strength
from us all.

Many are scared
and alone. A lot
feel like outcasts.
I have been there.
I don't want to go back
to that kind of life.

It's not really a life.
You just exist.

A Safe Place
BJ

My fingers cling to tree bark,
rough, ashy grey, some say white
lined in black—my tree is alive.
Sturdy, solid, long branchy arms
reach to the sky, where God lives.
Rough bark presses my cheek,
bringing kisses from someone
who loves me without judgment or restraint.

Rough bark accepts my tears
drizzling down each black outlined crack,
tears someone must surely feel with me.
So I cry again, to get them all out.
I feel warmth, sunshine oozing from my tree.
Looking up, I follow branch after branch
with my eyes, branch after branch,
reaching upward toward God, who loves
me most, pleading for me, praying arms;
each branch letting Him know
I need Him most right now.

Closing my eyes, I feel His comfort come
swooping in to hold me close, to save
me, to salvage my soul that
yearns to fly away
from this earthly world and all its pain.
I feel love and safety
consume my heart.

I lean back, exhausted,
against my tree, my connection with
someone who cares about me
and loves me most. Tree bark,
rough, shy grey, long branches
reach to the sky, where God lives.
This is my safe place. Against my tree.

20

BJ

Safe
Julie Scipio

Homeless is not safe.
I was brought up without safe.

I feel safe now
from all obstacles
because I have the right husband.

We will never, I pray, be homeless.
But, if "not safe" comes back,
I can find safety in Charles' arms.

Charles is strong and knows how
to protect. He is a hard worker.
He pays the rent.
He protects.

Charles reassures me,
"It's gonna be all right."
He calls me "Baby."

I am not worried.
I can see him now and hear his voice.
I am not afraid.

Home
Peg Butler

A day starts out at dawn,
gathering my stuff and pushing
a shopping cart containing
all my worldly possessions—
blankets, a few clothes, a dish
or two and a water bottle.

The cart is heavy and hard
to push. Cars honk at me
as I try to cross the street.

I dumpster dive for food
and other items that might
be of use for survival.
I can't leave my cart's side
as all my treasures
would quickly be stolen.

I find a corner to hold
up my sign:
HOMELESS ANYTHING
WOULD HELP.
A few people stop
and hand me a dime or two.
The change goes to the one
meal I'll have all day.

As night falls, the chill
in my tired bones
can be felt. I must find
a safe place for me and my cart.
I tie a rope around my ankle
and to the cart. Wrapping
myself in an old blanket,
I lay my head down, knowing
I made it through one more
day of homelessness.

Heart Words
Risa

My words are in my heart
  as a song and melody

that lifts high
  above the clouds

to the one
  who knows my heart

above all.
  They are within

my soul, ready,
    wanting

to speak truth,
    speak words that will

set men free
  and give them hope

words that will
    uplift.

Thanksgiving
eb

Heartbreak,
sweet among bitter,
good among bad,
endings after tumultuous beginnings.

Will there be a reckoning?
Will good and well-meaning people

get where they are going?
Does it matter anymore?

Do only evil and mean survive?
Is that the way to make it in the world?

Thanksgiving this year is barebones,
tremendous hope and tender mercies.

Surely there is reward to come;
we live in a magic world

with goodness at the corner
and providence like leaves.

We are magic creatures living
in a world with dimensions
designed just for us.

Who knows what is around the corner?
My love continues to be stretched…

The Gathering Place
Brenda Joyce Haynesworth

They open the doors of The Gathering Place and we rush into this sanctuary. We all enter knowing we will find a good breakfast, a place to take a nap and a place to greet and meet with friends in our community of women. We all have a common bond of loneliness and fear. I stare at the faces and see myself!

I'm the old White lady with the grey eyes, black dyed hair and the 60's bun on top of my head. There are wrinkles in my face from all the years of worrying about where I'm going to sleep tonight. I'm dressed and I look so professional, like I've got somewhere to go. But it's the bright pink lipstick on my thin lips and the orange polish on my long nails that gives way to the only signs that my mind is working hard to be normal.

I'm the lady who will strike up a conversation with my neighbor in the chair next to me. "This country is so advanced, but so behind! Are we still fighting in Vietnam? The new millennium came and went and the computers did not blow up! These damn kids have no respect! I hope they have those chili cheese dogs for lunch tomorrow—those were good!" I'm done with my diatribe, so I just bow my head and go back into my own world.

I'm the young Black woman who sits by myself, coat on in 80° weather, and little suitcase on wheels beside me, along with the big plastic bag with the remainder of all my earthly goods. Sitting and waiting with my chin in the palm of my hand, like the "thinking man" statue. My eyes are focused on one spot and I am so afraid that I will have to sleep on the streets again tonight. My mind and heart ache on the inside because no one I know really cares about the fact that I'm homeless. I look so silent and serene on the outside, but I'm crying and kicking and screaming on the inside.

I'm the old Native American woman who sits all alone observing the comings and goings of everyone else. My long, grey hair is just below my shoulders and belies the beauty of a past gone era. My hawk-like features and the wrinkles on my face say that I have weathered many a storm in my lifetime. I'm wise, strong and smart; so how in God's name did I get here? I know that if I think about it long enough, I can figure it out. And, when I do, you can be sure I will never pass this way again.

I'm the old Black lady pushing my walker, throwing out the "Hallelujahs" and "Praise God" to everyone. Singing my songs of salvation and grace not only brings me peace, but it is my way of sharing the blessings of God with everyone else. I know that if I can show them Jesus, if they can just learn to know the surpassing love of my God, they will not feel so bad about being lost and homeless. That's why I say, "God bless you," to everyone. Tears fall from my eyes and stream down my face, but it doesn't cause a big scene because everyone here knows why I'm crying. They just pass by, place a knowing hand on my shoulder and keep going. I am comforted by my comrades in this battle to survive. Well, PRAISE THE LORD!

I'm the young mother with three babies all under the age of four. No, they're not triplets. With the youngest on my hip, I take three cups to the juice counter, fill them with enough milk for each child and carry all three cups back to the table in one hand, using my fingers as tongs. Placing my baby in the high chair, I make sure each child is fed. I put cereal in the high chair tray for the youngest, but she keeps throwing it on the floor, along with orange slices I've placed there already. As soon as they are done eating, all three are going to the kids' area so I can take a breather.

I'm the more mature woman who has been in this place way too long. I'm beginning to get sick and tired of this situation of being homeless for more than two years. I scream on the inside to my Holy Father in heaven, "PLEASE RESCUE ME!" I have so much love to give, but no one will ever know because my circumstances have become a barrier to my friends and family. They ignore me and have cast me out of their lives, as if by doing so they will be untouched by the stigma of homelessness. I hold on to my faith in Jesus because I know He will deliver me. And He does! I now have my own apartment, with an air mattress as my only piece of furniture. I hang a small, framed picture on the wall; I'M HOME!

I'm the lady walking around the lobby on my cane, yelling at the top of my voice, "HAS ANYONE SEEN MY WAL-MART BAG?" All I did was go to the bathroom for a minute and come back to my seat to find my bag gone! The people who work here, who are walking through the lobby at the time, help me look around for it. Even the other clients look around their seats, but my bag is nowhere to be found. I go back to the Resource Desk to inquire about my bag, but it's not there. I come back and stand in the lobby again, "HAS ANYONE SEEN MY WAL-MART BAG?" A worker behind the Welcome desk tells me that's why we have the rule to keep your belongings with you at all times. I look at her with a scowl on my face; to hell with the rules. "HAS ANYONE SEEN MY WAL-MART BAG?"

I'm the middle-aged Black woman who's still walking around in shock by being unemployed and homeless. I walk up to the Welcome desk and tell the lady there that I don't know why I'm here. I don't even know what services they can offer. I guess I had that "deer in the headlights" look on my face, because she tells me all about the services. She gives me a form to complete, and when I return it, she asks me if I want to eat some breakfast. I learn I can take a shower and wash my clothes. I can go to the art room and stir my creative juices. I can go to the computer lab and stay in touch with my friends and family by email. I can even get help creating a resume. And I find my greatest release in my writing class, where women just like me get a chance to put on paper the cries of their heart. I am no longer feeling abandoned and discouraged. Even though I still don't have a "home," I am not "less," because I am a client of The Gathering Place.

We Are
Peg Butler

We are the cold
and the wandering people.

From street to street
we walk, nowhere to go,
no place to call home.

We wonder where the next
meal is coming from.
We are lonely and afraid

of another dark, snowy night,
with no place to lay our heads
that is safe.

We are a lost population,
with no rights or respect.
We have feelings of loneliness
and feelings of abandonment.

We really are strong,
for we endure,
no matter what people say.

We are the homeless,
with no address, no name.

We are calling out loud
with every cold breath we take.
Give us a place in society

so we can belong.

Brooke Meadow

Auction
eb

Time to go! Come on…
moving down lines of cars.

The same characters are there,
people with a few hours to spend
on a Wednesday to make a couple of bucks.

They all know each other;
gossip in the temp service
is rampant, like wildfire.

Different ones
are getting old there.

Connected

Sandina Tanguma

I am surrounded by beautiful, strong women who tell me, tell all, their stories.
I am so blessed and feel I am meant to be here to hear them.

Open your heart: feel, connect.

Watch the tri-colored leaves of green, burnt orange, and yellow
In their state of transformation.

You are in a state of transformation
Everything you see, hear and experience was meant for you.

Feel the wind, take a breath,
And just be.

Point out the shapes and make your own pictures
From the elements of the world.

Tread the earth and grow things in it.
Care for it and change it.

Feel the boundless textures:
The rough tree bark, the gritty sand, the silky water.

Reach out and take in.
Embrace!

Find the flower hidden in the shadow of a city building.
Expand your mind.

Hope, inspire and support.
You were created to do wonders!

Thank You
Leticia D. Tanguma

Two women, argue, escalating, their voices, angry. It's sad that it was during a time we were all eating lunch. For some, maybe, that's the first time they've eaten that day, or, that week.

You came, pregnant, and firmly told them to calm down. You cook for us. Your family waits at home. Your feet are tired.

I came in after working all week for a temp agency, where I witnessed and experienced the bosses' sexist comments and verbal abuse. I had scraped three day old gunk off dirty pans. I had walked a hundred miles, back and forth, through fancy carpeted exhibit halls and cement basement mazes, all for the gluttonous patrons. I got lost many times. At the end of the week, when I went to get my check, the temp agency said, "Yours is not ready. Come back on Monday." I don't have money for food for the weekend.

"How are you doing?" you ask as you hand me a plate for Friday afternoon snack,

"Okay," I say. "I'm glad I get to eat this food. I don't have much food for the weekend. I was going to buy some, but they didn't have my check ready."

I sat down to eat, enjoying the food. All of a sudden, you came and plopped a large paper bag with handles, on the table. It was filled with food: spinach, tomatoes, bread, tuna fish, candy, soup. It was more than enough for the weekend, until I could come back on Monday and eat again at The Gathering Place.

"Thank you!"

Risa

Inspiration
BJ

Being true to myself always comes to mind when I think about inspiration.

Being a Lakota woman, I struggle to fit into the expectations and social mores of a dominant society. My way of thinking, feeling and processing information is quite different from others around me. I do not have the same values or beliefs that many others have, even though I've grown up in the same schools, lived in similar neighborhoods and worked together with others to make the world—even if it's just my small community circles—a better place for my children, all children, and our future generations.

Don't get me wrong—I am not saying I don't have feelings or emotions or worries, thoughts or cares like everyone else in the world—just that, culturally and genetically, I believe my spirit, my heart, and my brain are simply wired differently. You might say I am a Mac to your PC.

Whenever I do anything to try to fit in with others around me, dominant society, or attempt to change my way of thinking to conform with the norm, I create an imbalance within myself that becomes very uncomfortable to live with, that often leads to depression and feelings of deep failure. When I was much younger, this left me feeling like I was always on the outside looking in, like I didn't know how to be like other people, even to the point of feeling like I was a failure at life.

Fortunately, as I've gotten older, and the need to fit in and conform to a way of life that is foreign to my system is losing its grip on me, I've found that my greatest inspiration comes from letting go of outside expectations and simply being true to myself!

Being true to myself means loving and holding my family, my Tiyospaye, close to my heart and not letting them go. Having a full pot of soup or spaghetti on the stove, ready for even those who might come by for an "unexpected" visit, keeping my extra pillows and blankets in the closet for those who traveled a long way to see me.

Being true to myself means being ready to take a stand for what I believe in, to show my kids and grandkids that good things and a good life are worth standing up and fighting for. To teach by my example, to speak from the heart, to be honest and follow through on what I say. Also, to be ready to tell a story, whether my own story or that of another, and weave an uplifting lesson into it that will be remembered by young, impressionable minds.

Being true to myself means being ready to go at the drop of a hat to help someone else who needs my help, to cook for the community when needed, or asked, and giving what little I do have to someone who needs it more. It means handing over a sandwich, a quarter, or a helping hand, not because it was asked or begged of me, but because I see the need.

Being true to myself means living my thanks to the Creator for giving me such a beautiful world to live in with everything I need to survive and to live with joy, each and every day. To live my thanks with laughter and a sense of humor, to express my happiness as the Creator wants me to be happy. And then to give back, because I know it is true what the Creator taught my people, that as long as we take care of each other, we will live long upon the earth.

Being true to myself is the inspiration that makes me feel balanced and complete.

My Biggest Regret
Paula Cordier

It's a brisk fall morning, with leaves floating from trees onto the pavement below, only to get lost among many shoes. People in business suits rush to and fro, the early morning hustle and bustle of the 16th Street Mall.

My morning appointment taken care of, I'm on my way to catch a bus home. Four food stamp dollars in my pocket, I wander into Walgreens to browse for a snack and waste some minutes until the bus comes.

A whole package of frosted cinnamon rolls for 99¢--what a deal! I pick up a quart of milk for another 99¢. I missed breakfast and I love cinnamon rolls.

Leaving the store in the direction of my bus, I'm pulled up short by the sight I see in the alleyway. He's scruffy and dirty, with an unkempt beard, sleeping in a sitting position on top of his rolled-up sleeping bag.

Everyone is walking past, not glancing in his direction, pretending he isn't there. I see him. I see the lines in his well-worn face. I see his weariness from living such a harsh existence, the weariness in his body and shoulders.

I look down at the cinnamon rolls I was so eager to eat. I look back at him. He doesn't know I'm there. He's too exhausted to care.

I know he must be hungry. Not hungry—he's probably starving. I want to give him my milk and cinnamon rolls, but I get scared. What if he rejects my offering? What if he curses at me for waking him? What if he takes his anger at the world out on me?

I feel like a coward as I creep past him to my destination. I look back at him and hate myself for being afraid. I had two more food stamps for more cinnamon rolls. My bus comes and I get on to go home. I'm hungry and can't get that man out of my head. I open cinnamon rolls that are still delicious as I eat them with tears running down my face. The milk is ice cold.

All these years later, my biggest regret is not going up to him and saying, "Here, these are for you…"

Heart
Kim Holder

In the center of
my chest, between
my breasts, is a wagon;
in it is my heart.

Within this wagon, it has been
jostled, pulled, slid, pushed,
hidden, tugged, parked, driven,
seated and thrust.

Heart of mine speaks now,
wishes to be heard and felt.
Heart not only has a voice
but also heart has eyes.

Heart can see others' hearts,
dark, twisted, light, open,
broken, crying, screaming, closed,
silent, singing, whole, speaking.

Heart to heart,
bring me to live through
my heart.

Heart of mine in the center
of my chest,
sits in a wagon, waiting.

The Face of Homelessness and Hope
Jennie K. Foster

Our bed is under a bush with a dirty blanket for warmth. Our kitchen is a dumpster near our bed. The food is dirty and rotten, yet it fills our stomachs. Our toilet is a wall or under a tree. When it's cold outside we are cold. When it's hot therc is no relief for us. Every day we walk the streets with no place to go.

We are not alone in our journey; we are many people that the mainstream doesn't want to look upon. To them, we are a useless lot. They wonder why we don't help ourselves. Many of them wonder what happened to us that we ended up on the streets. They believe the problem is drugs, alcohol or mental illness. These are a few reasons why we are homeless. Then there are those of us who have been battered, lost our jobs, the roofs over our heads, our children, with no money left in our pockets. We are destined for the streets, the bushes and the dumpsters.

Before we became street people, we had dreams. Sometimes our dreams were of family, home, a job so that we could support our families. Life isn't our dreams. We became ill, unable to work. Our bills become delinquent. We can't pay our rent and are evicted with nowhere to go. Standing on the street for hours, a shelter takes us in for the night. One night there is no room for us. Depression looms in the darkness of our minds. We begin to walk the streets again.

We desire clean food, a roof over our heads, clean clothes, clean toilet facilities, an opportunity to make a living, a place where we can start a new life.

In the depths of our lives on the streets, feeling hopeless, useless and forgettable, a thought might creep into our minds. The thought is God. If we aren't able to help ourselves, maybe someone would want to help us. In the corner of a concrete wall and behind a bush we fall to our knees and cry in prayer. Death is at our door. Our lives have been so difficult that we think perhaps if we surrender to a spiritual power there may be hope. Sleep creeps into that teary spot under the bushes; when we awaken, it is a perfect morning. The sky is blue and the weather wonderful. As we walk the streets that we walked the day before, in our hearts there is hope that today will bring a better life.

If you understood our lives, would you help us?

Leticia D. Tanguma

Panicked
C.M. Davidson-Sole

Heart racing, body tensing,
breathing labored and hard.

Blood boiling, head pulsating,
things are going wrong.

Wait a minute! Wait a minute!
I can't catch my breath!
Palms are sweaty, upset stomach,
I'm gonna lose my lunch.
If I don't get a grip
on myself, I'm going
to explode.

I'm a scared little rabbit caught
in a wave of panic every day.
I can't turn here, I can't run there.
Oh God, I'm always scared.

Being panicked ain't no fun,
you're always on the run.
I'd like to feel, just this once,
that panic's days are done.

Anger and Peace
Leticia D. Tanguma

Anger shoved through the door wearing soaked bandages and torn rags, looked around and shouted, "Why have you left the child?"

The others, adorned with precious gems and plastic faces, heard the voice of Anger, but did not turn around to look, for they had already put money in the homeless meter, volunteered in the soup line once a week, and gave a portion of their earnings to the local crisis center once a month. They smiled and complimented each other's portfolios and arranged rendezvous of golf and shopping sprees.

Peace crawled through the door, naked, hungry and cold. Barely able to move, Peace whispered something.

If any were curious about what Peace said, it soon passed. They were happy they did not have to change a thing.

Part I: What Happened?
Hilda Miera

Here I am; it's a first for me—I'm homeless. I'm around women at The Gathering Place all the time. I see what they go through—the tears, the hardships of living on the streets or in shelters. I always knocked on wood or thanked God for not having to be in that situation. But, here I am—homeless.

It's been so stressful having to move my things out, having them spread out here and there—storage, neighbors, friends. How did I get here? It happened so fast. Almost like a blink of my eyes. Boom—homeless.

I was scared, stressed, just the word made me cry. I've never been such a crybaby. But, I knew I had The Gathering Place. I can do this, I keep telling myself—I'll be OK. No, I'm not as strong as I used to be. I looked in the mirror! Stop it—you can do this—you're still strong—maybe not physically, but mentally you are! Stop, you're going to be OK. It's only going to be 'til you find a place.

Buckle up!! Two months, you can find a place. At least you have your Section 8. You have no monies, but at least you have that. There is a light at the end of this tunnel. You have to believe that. First things first.

Move my stuff out. Finally, it's done. I had so much. Now it's just enough to start over. The rest got thrown out. I'm told that the same people who caused all these problems at home were like vultures going through my things. Two women fighting over a bra—that's funny. My friends said it made them sick to see how they were acting. It's OK—it's another day.

My first night homeless I spent with my best friend (that's what she is to me—I hope she knows that). We watched a movie and I was able to unwind and sleep for the first time in a couple of weeks because of the stress. I went downstairs and told her how I sat on the edge of the bed and said, out loud to myself, "So this is what it's like being homeless!" We laughed.

OK, time to go to TGP. Make calls, see how this shelter thing works. I'm so scared. I don't know what to expect. Do we get there, go to bed, get up and leave and start over? I'm nervous.

I'm at The Delores House. Wow, it looks like a nice place. I'm in—I'm relieved—it's a very nice place. Am

42

I in the right place? Something's being lifted off my shoulders—all that weight of the stress. I'm going to be OK, I can handle this. It's nothing at all like I expected. It's going to be OK. I'll try to get a permanent bed for as long as I need. It could happen tonight, tomorrow, next week, but it will happen.

I see so many familiar faces. I feel safe. I can do this.

Part II: Home Sweet Home
Hilda Miera

It's been three and a half months since I became homeless.

Homeless. I can say the word and not be ashamed or embarrassed. I'm homeless! So many good things have come out of all this. I'm not saying it hasn't been hard or frustrating, because God knows it has been. I knew there was a reason why all this was happening; I just did not know it at the time.

My first month was so hard. Not knowing if you were going to be able to stay another night at the same shelter, a different shelter, a friend's house or on the street somewhere. All the running back and forth just to sign up for a bed, dragging your stuff around, calling at a certain time to only hear, "Sorry, we're all filled up, try again tomorrow."

So many times, I would cry out loud, "I can't do this anymore. I just can't." But, after a good cry, I'd wipe my tears and tell myself, you're gonna be OK, tomorrow's another day. My last day at the Aristocrat. What am I going to do? I used my twelve days. Meeting so many people, moving in and out. People on meds for bipolar, depression, anxiety, stress, so many different faces. Some good, some bad. Some use you and some help you. All the drama and gossip. When does it stop? You're up, you're down. Please help me get through this.

I wasn't gonna call the number she gave me, but something inside said call. Why, I wondered? I have a bed for one more night. They'll only say call back tomorrow. I called. She said, "Yes, we have a bed. Call me back in fifteen minutes." I was shaking. I was crying. A bed for thirty days. Thank you, God. I called back. She asked questions, I answered. Her last question, "Are you a veteran?" "Yes," I replied. She went on to say they had nine beds put aside for homeless vets and a program to help us get back on our feet and we could stay longer. I was so emotional I couldn't speak. She told me when to come by.

As I walked in the door, I prayed and I asked my mom, who had passed, to help me and be with me because I needed her more than ever. I walked through the door. It was a nice place. As I looked past the counter, on a bulletin board, there she was: Katie. All these drawings done by children who had stayed. Before me, and the one that stood out, was one of a little girl. She wrote her name in all these wonderful colored glitter pens: KATIE. My mother's name. She was here with me. I felt my heart jump, I swallowed the lump in my throat and tried to keep the tears from swelling in my eyes. I was home for now. My mom was with me. I knew I would be safe here. There was a reason I was here.

They treat us good here. They feed us, give us a bed, give us a place to rest and not worry about the next night and so on and so on. The stress was lifted from my shoulders. I felt the peace in my heart and soul. Thank you, God, for bringing me here, for guiding me from place to place to wind up here. All we have to do is follow the rules, do our chores and start getting things in order so we can get done what we have to do. Get our lives back on track. That end of the tunnel is getting closer. Good things are starting to happen. That light is getting brighter!

VAL

Part III: My Bright Light
Hilda Miera

I'm not homeless anymore! It feels so good to say that. I've reached the end of my tunnel. The light is so bright. I always knew it would come. It's strange (or not) how things happen. There's a reason for everything that happens and how and when it happens in our lives.

I know it sounds strange when I say, "So many good things happened to me being homeless," but it's true. Once I wound up at the Brandon Center, only good things came my way. I found out I had Veterans' Benefits. I received my medical needs at the VA. I'm getting counseling for my PTSD. I go to classes, which are helping me understand how PTSD affects your life. My dental needs are being met. I also lost weight. The first month was sixteen pounds due to the stress—not a good way to lose. The rest from keeping busy and being happy and not having to worry about having a place to sleep. My total weight loss is thirty-four pounds and counting.

I got reunited with my sisters; we hadn't talked or seen each other in nine years. We've let the past go and now it's just going forward. My younger sister and my niece have really been there for me. It feels so good to have family in my life again. A couple of weeks ago, I ran into my daughter on the bus. I saw her and my granddaughter for the first time in a year and a half. She gave me her number. It's a start. She said my other granddaughter is always asking about me. I can't wait 'til I see her. We were so close. I miss them very much.

I got discharged from the Brandon Center for, as I would say, trying to help new people. I would explain how they wanted us to do things such as chores. Some women appreciated this and some called me bossy or being a mother hen. Staff said not to change, because they knew I had a good heart and it was part of my personality. It was sad to leave the Brandon Center, but, from there I went to Theo (Theodora House). I know there's a reason for all this. Now it's just like the regular shelters. Be up at 6 a.m. and out at 8 a.m. We can come back between 5 p.m. 'til 9 p.m. I thank God I still have a place to sleep. A warm place to be. I moved in Wednesday night. Thursday, I applied for SSDI and SSI. Friday, I went bright and early to apply at a complex for disabled and elderly. I had everything I needed with me. (My doctor at the VA signed my Med 9 for my disability. It had taken me 2-1/2 years of going to clinics and never getting it signed, or getting the proper care and medicine I needed.) I got home (the shelter) at 5:30 p.m. I had a note to come sign my lease on Saturday at 9 a.m. I ran downstairs to the TV room, where I was sleeping on an airbed until a bed opened up, and yelled out to the girls, "I got an apartment!" It felt so good. I had tears in my eyes. I could have moved in Saturday night, but Sunday we had signed up for a "Mothers' Day in December" thing they were having for the women at Brandon and Theodora House. I had to stay for that. I told the girls, "I can take one more night in the TV room." On Saturday, an organization brought over a Christmas dinner for us. It was a great day. Sunday, I went to church with my friend, Sharon. I saw my old friends at church. At prayer request and praise, I announced I wasn't homeless any more. I praised God for helping me get through the last five months and ten days. I asked for prayer for all the other women I met at the shelter that good things would also come to them. I thanked God for being with me and watching over me through my time of homelessness.

Back to Brandon Center for my Mothers' Day. It was wonderful. I had my hair cut and styled, my nails done, my eyebrows waxed and makeup done. We got to pick out two outfits and had a wonderful day of good food. The lady who did nails, Mary Sue, gave me the best hug ever—long and so caring. She wished me the best after I told her my story and how I just found an apartment.

It's over now, time to go home. I packed my stuff and realized I couldn't make it on the bus with everything. So, I called myself a cab and went home.

This Way, This Way
eb

It's the spirit,
though the body declines
and has ailments
and aches and pains.

We are more than that.
We are more
than this water sack
we occupy.

More? you ask.
One body?
How can I be more?
What will happen when I go?

How can I be more?

We all have something to deliver,
something shiny
and brand new to give.
We are shiny,
shiny bright.

What you have to give
the best, brightest person
may not have.
We are all special and unique.

And we do live on.
The world is a different place
because of us,
and when we go on,
we leave a wrinkle
where we were.

We are not forgotten,
We are here today!
We leave a mark;
the world is not the same.

People are not the same,
positively or negatively.
The world is a new place
because
we've been there.

In that way, we live on,
through other people.

I imagine that the stars
peeking through the sky
are souls gone on;
the Bible says we have
a great audience.

A God who calls
the billions of stars by name?
A planet that belittles
earth to a dot?
An angel who says,
when asked his name,
"It is beyond
your understanding."

Yes, yes. This way, this way,
spirit whispers.
We are all old souls.
We are more;

the body expires
but the spirit triumphs!
And rises
and smiles at another day.

We are more.

Alone
Peg Butler

Being homeless for a woman means often being alone. Whether it be in the day or night, danger lurks around each corner.

I was sitting at a bus stop in the middle of the day when a man approached me from behind and wrapped his arms around my neck, yelling unclear words in my ears. I felt his strong arms pull at my throat and was unsure if he was going to release me. I was alone, with no one around to help.

I began to scream, "Get away from me! Get away from me!" He released his grip and began to laugh, and then this stranger darted across the street, yelling unclear words and gesturing in my direction.

I realized that a single woman, even in the middle of the day, has to be aware of her surroundings. Being alone and looking defenseless is an open door to anyone coming along and taking advantage of you.

I now carry a whistle and stand up at the bus stops, making sure no strange men are lurking around the corner.

Living as a homeless woman without any walls means being extra aware of who is around you any time of the day or night. Dangers for women are out there and you'd better beware.

Hungry
Verna K. Nahulu

He rarely looks up; his wife sits beside him.
He holds their sign:

HUNGRY…HAVING A HARD TIME…
ANYTHING HELPS. PLEASE.

I had $4 in a ball in my purse.
My fingers searched the bottom and found it.
Here you go—enjoy!"
The woman thanked me and scurried on
to get something to eat. She returned
and shared morsels with her husband.
They closed their eyes in thanks, and I saw a tear
glisten on his face as I acknowledged them,
and crossed the street.

My thoughts wandered to a Bible verse:
"I was hungry and you fed me;
I was naked and you clothed me."
My eyes filled with tears as I remembered their faces.

Hunger stings…stings so bad.
I looked back one more time.
They followed me with their eyes,
and I could hear their thoughts:
Thank you kind lady,
and thank you, God.

WHERE IS HOME?
Paula Cordier

Home is so long ago that, decades later, all that remains are the bittersweet memories, growing hazy with age. Home is the smell of sweet grass, carried by sharp, crisp South Dakota winds through my grandmother's open window while I snuggled beneath handmade quilts to take a nap.

Home is knowing who I am with certainty, and being proud that I am Indian, even though I get teased and picked on for being "white." Home is my grandmas, grandpa, aunts, uncles, and cousins, a community where I belong.

Home is a great big blue sky stretched over rolling hills and grassland that you can see for miles. Home is waking up from my nap to find a tiny flowered wreath for me to wear on my head, made by a fairy. My three year old eyes widen with wonder as my mother's secret smile lights up her eyes.

Home is powwows lasting into the night. I excitedly run into the arena with my homemade shawl, sewn lovingly by grandmother's hands. I have no fear or self-consciousness as I move my tiny feet to the beat of drums. It is where I belong. Home is following in my mother's footsteps in the dusty dirt, eating sunflower seeds under the hot sun.

Home is a land filled with black hair and brown skin. Even though my hair is a lighter shade and my skin paler, it is where I belong. I have to defend my place, to rough little kids who call me "white" like it's a curse, but it is where I belong.

Sharon Kumm

Richest of the Rich
BJ

In 1995, on the day I was laid off from my job, I got hit by a car that ran a red light. The driver tossed "his" license out of the window and then sped off. It turned out to be stolen, so there was no insurance coverage for the injuries to my pelvis. The doctor said I would need physical therapy and couldn't work for four months.

I had to apply for Medicaid and felt fortunate to be covered. But I dreaded the thought of applying for welfare. For me, it has been a "Catch 22" experience—difficult to get and even more difficult to get off of. Instead, I used my last check to pay what basic bills I could ahead of time and then applied for food stamps, so we could ride out this difficult time.

When I had to explain these things to my children, I thought they would be hurt and disappointed. I was worried they would miss the little luxuries we'd had, like an occasional night at the movies, or eating out, or a new item of clothing that they actually needed. Instead, their response was upbeat and positive. My daughter, 12, told me, "Don't worry Mom, we don't need movies or new clothes right now," while my son, 10, said, "At least we're not homeless. And we can help you now, too."

They're just kids, I thought. They might not understand how serious our situation is. Yet they proved true to their word, while the Creator sent opportunities and blessings our way to help us survive.

There was a woman, a friend of a friend, who lived down the street from us. Out of the blue, she called and explained how she felt her three-year-old son was old enough to be left with a sitter my daughter's age, and would I mind if she sat with him so she could go out with her friends occasionally. Not even knowing our situation at home, she paid my daughter well every time she babysat. And in turn, my daughter would buy herself or her brother a new pair of shoes, or a pair of jeans. She became very adept at saving money and planning ahead.

Meanwhile, in my son's class at school, the kids earned rewards for their work and participation in class that were handed out every Friday. Suddenly there were no more complaints about homework! And every Friday, instead of choosing a small toy for himself, he faithfully chose the "penny" candy. Then, he would rush home to stand before me, proudly holding out the pieces in his grubby little boy hand, explaining what he'd done that week to earn such a windfall.

He offered me the best piece first, and I could do nothing but give his gift dignity by taking it. Then, he'd offer his sister first choice before taking one for himself. Hiding tears at his loving contribution, I knew, as he knew, that this was way better than eating out. To this day, he still does his best in school and has a tendency to take risks by taking challenging classes and by doing things that go against his normally shy nature, like emceeing for the school's choir program.

I can't recall the small details of how we actually made it through those four months without a basic income. But, I will always remember the large details, those that came from my children's big hearts as they kept their promise to help me.

Poverty and wealth are only a state of mind. We might be the poorest of the poor, yet we can also feel the richest of the rich! Hardship and struggle can actually be blessings from the Creator to help us become better human beings. At the same time, comfort and wealth might actually serve the same purpose. Rather than being a blessing for a life well-lived, or because God loves you more, it might actually be your own personal test to see what you will do with yourself in spite of it!

At any rate, for myself, I know that my 12-year-old's trip to the shoe store with her little brother and my 10-year-old's simple offering of penny candy are worth more to me than a million bucks any day!

Abuse
N.A.S.

I am a senior and a Colorado native, and have experienced so much in my life! A battered wife, accused of everything that he would bully me with. Total falsehoods, i.e. myself having affairs. Finally, when our youngest was fourteen years old, my husband was drunk so much of the time that he punched this young adult son down a flight of stairs.

That did it for me! Clarity came to me. God did not place myself and four young adults to take any more abuse, not any one of these very specially great kids I had worked very hard to raise.

I filed for divorce. Back that many years ago, women were labeled "displaced homemakers." Thank God, today it is we, both women and men, can say what it actually is. We are abused!

Where Is Home?

eb

It's a precarious state of being
Wanting to show my situation and its test.
It's a place where you can see exactly who and what you really are.

On TV, I heard someone say
"You are who you are with."

Iron levels low, nutrition low, income low,
Surely this is not who I am!

No!
This is not what I've dreamed or planned for.

But, tottering, hovering, wobbling, swaying, perched on another precipice,
I'm a "teeter totter" rocking on a pointy support.

Where do I go from here? Hang on baby?
It ain't much but it's all I've got.

Thank you people, every one, for those appreciative nods and
Words of kind encouragement.

They mean a lot to me.
I feel so undeserving to receive so much.

But watch! If it is the end of me
I will repay or die trying.

I want to give back even though right now I have nothing.
I give what I can: a full heart and mind.

Want to. Want to.
Does this mean anything?

Honey
BJ

My two small children and I wearily walked into the bus station carrying our few belongings. The trip had been long and difficult for them. I'd run out of money the day before and could only buy a loaf of bread and a jar of peanut butter for the last leg of it, and they were still hungry.

"Don't worry," I told them, "we're almost there."

Fishing out one of our last quarters, I called my sister. I was not prepared for her words.

"My husband doesn't think it's a good idea to help you. I'm sorry. I can't let you stay with us."

Hurt, I asked for our mother's number, only to hear, "Mom said to tell you that she can't keep you either. Her apartment's too small. I hope you'll understand."

I told her, "I don't have any money to stay anywhere else, or to even feed my kids! Can't we come over so they can eat?"

"I'm sorry," she said again. "It's my husband… I can't…"

Click.

NO, I didn't want to understand! I'd traveled all this way because they invited me to come to Denver to make a fresh start after domestic violence shattered my home. They overwhelmed me with all the opportunities to go to school and find work. They told me they missed us and said we could stay with them until I could get on my feet.

Now we were left stranded at the bus station! I looked at the faces of my unsuspecting children. I never could have imagined in a million years that I would be facing this desperate dilemma. Where would I put them to sleep that night? How would I feed them? Visions of bus benches and alleys brought choking tears to my throat.

I realized that what I did next would be crucial, because I needed to get them to a safe place before dark. I prayed that I would find help before my quarters ran out. Paging through the phone book, I found a listing of shelters and called one. "I'm sorry, but we're full." I felt crushed and defeated. "But, listen," she went on, "try SafeHouse. It sounds like that's the place you need to call anyway."

Preparing myself for the worst, I called the number for SafeHouse and began my story. "Oh, Honey," a warm voice soothed, "you and your babies have been through so much. Look, I'm sending a cab right over. It's going to pick you up at the main entrance, so be out there waiting, okay?" Wow! And I didn't even get around to asking if they had room for us!

As soon as we arrived, we were shuttled into the dining room, where supper was still laid out, and encouraged us to eat all we wanted. Then we were given towels and bedding and shown to our room. Oh, what luxury! I would have been happy for just a tiny corner to lay our heads down, yet they gave us so much more, especially their kindness and concern! Instead of an alley or a bus bench, I tucked my freshly bathed kids into bed that night between the sweetest smelling sheets on earth! They were truly in a safe place.

While we lived there, I was mentored in the ways of the world—where to go to apply for welfare, housing, schools for my kids and myself, and how to ride the bus. They helped me map out my own plan of self-sufficiency and stood behind me as I tracked my goals and successfully met them. And I was happy for the opportunity to do simple household chores. It meant a lot to have a floor to sweep and dishes to wash during that difficult "homeless" time. And when we moved into our own home, we were given furniture and household items that I'd "earned" by doing the chores I'd found comfort in.

SafeHouse and the wonderful people that work there give the healing gift of involvement and action that builds self-esteem. My family may have seemed cold, but to this day I will always thank God for a stranger's voice that called me "Honey."

So, thank you, SafeHouse, and all of you wonderful people everywhere who work on behalf of women like me. Thank you for your kindness that soothes a hurting "Honey's" heart and keeps us safe until we can stand on our feet again.

Day by Day
Rogene Munnell

I thank the Lord
for each day, and hope
for a closer walk
with him/her. I pray
every day.

Every day is an opportunity
to care for yourself
and spend time with others.

I have heard it said
that it is not wise to dwell
too much in the past,
nor worry too much
about the future

for we have only the present
in which to live.

Kay L. Eshelman

Home?

Pepper-Lee

Tearing through these streets,
accepting atrocious defeats,

with meager means and hopeful dreams
of simply being able to eat.

Prayerfully striving to survive through each day,
barbarically scrounging for a bed in which to lay.

Addicts, scoundrels and perils of all sorts,
ambitions and ideals we just tend to simply abort.

Friends, fiends, enemies and cohorts,
isolatingly alone, cold inabilities to fathom a beginning to court.

Cries and screams, and bloodthirsty mongrels
feel just like the beginning to the end, with reality a mere feeling,
lying within.

Eyes open wide shut; variations of hearts going hard and dark,
purity of life's goodness seeming to be a simple glimmer or light spark.

In just others, it seems to shine, and shine very boldly;
in the warriors of the street, this light seems to shine dimly and quite lonely.

These battles and wars call soldiers from ALL walks of humanity,
and you never know who'll walk the front lines, never can tell,
not truly or wholeheartedly.

Writers, superstars, all members through societies
indeed have been stricken with this powerful rod known as poverty.

How Do You Reach Out When You Are In a Hole?
Leticia D. Tanguma

How do you reach out
    when you are in a hole?

How do you share a meal
    when you have none?
How do you stop a friend from dying
    of drugs, of drink, of loneliness
    when you are gasping for breath?
How do you invite someone in
    when you don't have a house?

Here it is real.
    Each face has kindness and hope
although they live on the streets,
    although they live in a shelter,
        although they have been beaten down
            by angry men,
              by poverty,
                by lack of luck.

Here it is real, as each one with care reaches
    out to her sister,
        crying in agony, who has not been
        recognized for
            her own beauty
              or worth.

Each one shares her message of dignity.

That is how you reach out
    when you are in a hole.

Claim
Sandina Tanguma

What should I claim? What would I claim?
The first thing that comes to mind is water—
its blue and biting power—its motion—
its ability to cleanse—to wash away—
to spread out—to be deep—to swallow
secrets—to be raged by storms, and to be
calm after—to give life—to be a part
of every human being—to be clear—
reflecting—a raindrop to a river to the sea—
to be absorbed by the earth—to travel
upwards again and to fall—to gather in
the clouds before releasing,
and, though I claim it,
the water is not only my own,
for the likeness of the stars is cast
in water.

I claim that piece of earth over there,
the one that's been trampled and uncared for,
the one where nothing grows.
I'm gonna plant something there—a beginning—
and see what emerges, what returns to me to be
shared. I'm gonna build something on that earth too—build
it strong—and even if they come to knock it down—or I
make it tremble from within—it won't fall.

I claim myself as a little girl, and I
hold her and tell her, "You'll make it."

VAL

You've Got to Move On
C.M. Davidson-Sole

You've lost your health, you have no job,
you can't pay your mortgage or rent.
They've got to foreclose, they've got to evict;
it's enough to make you lament.
Then come the words so cruel, so wrong:
"YOU'VE—GOT—TO—MOVE—ON!"

The angry, hard wooden nightstick, part of police battlements, strikes a blunt, painful blow to my ankle. "Hey, you! You can't sleep in this park! You're trespassing on public property! You can't stay here! You've got to move on."

The cold, hard ground digs into my side. "It's not so bad sleeping under this bridge with my piece of cardboard to cover up with," I reassure myself on a cold, snowy January night. A bright, intrusive flashlight pierces the night sky, stinging my tired, bloodshot eyes. "Hey, you! It's dangerous sleeping down here! You're trespassing! You've got to move on."

Daytime comes, still the abuse drones on, with no relief in sight. Walking around downtown Denver is no joy, but what else can you do with no money or no transportation?

My legs are swollen, my ankles are throbbing. I find a spot to sit down and begin my embarrassing plea. "Hey, mister, hey, ma'am, can you spare some change?"

"Go get a job, you lazy bitch!" yells a passing man. The biting words from a bitter man cut deep in my spirit as I continue my plea with just a bit less confidence than before.

I stop into a nearby McDonald's to use the restroom. The manager hones in on me like a hawk searching for its prey. "Hey, you! You can't use our facilities unless you are A PAYING CUSTOMER! You can't stay here or we will call the police! You've got to move on!"

I've found it! A shelter has room for me! YAHOO! PRAISE GOD! I can finally get some rest!"

Not so fast. It's not going to last. I've only got a 30-day stay.

RULES OF THE SHELTER:
1. Overnight only
2. Be up by six, and, oh, by the way,
3. You've chores in store, so hit the floor.
4. You've got to leave by eight.
5. You can't come back 'til six at night.
6. Curfew is at nine.

Don't blame me, it's the shelter's rules. Really, they're not mine. And, if you can't live by these rules, my friend, we'll have to demand you get out!

You've lost your health, you have no job,
you can't pay your mortgage or rent.
They've got to foreclose, they've got to evict;
it's enough to make you lament.

And so the cadence of homelessness goes; it keeps marching on and on.
Hey families, hey singles, and hey little ones too, get up! You've got to move on.

They Were Hungry
Brooke Meadow

They were never so hungry
as last Thanksgiving week.
Hungry for something to eat,
starving for somewhere to go,
aching for a smile that's sweet.
They were never so hungry
as Thanksgiving week.

You know who they are,
who don't fit in,
who live on a smile and grin,
who, oh so alone
when families feast, suffering
politics of separation and fear.

The dysfunctional pattern
well-worn and clear,
they feed on the goodwill
of a stranger
at the bus stop or sidewalk,
out on the street
when someone they greet
doesn't know the unwritten rule
from family perception:

You're not okay,
or worth my time of day.

Great to See

eb

Great to see
  those on the street
  usually out struggling
  inside
  sober
  working on computers

Great to see
  one saddened by loss
  beginning a new chapter,
  caring for a grandchild
  of a loved one
  now gone.

Great to see
  happy, welcoming faces,
  new art supplies,
  soft voices not needing to yell.

Great to see
  others believing in you,
  expecting you to succeed;
  instill a feeling of well-being;
  you will be fine.

Winter Shelter
VAL

I can see in the far distance
a long procession of people,
all dancing in place,
while steam radiates
out of their nostrils
and mouths
as they wait to enter
a welcoming warmth
where the worries
of cold have to wait
outside the door.

My eyes can see
the wonderful white snow
as I walk quickly,
not to let the winter chill
seep through my attire.
My feet keep moving
closer to that next building.
This aged body
has not given up,
as long as the heat
is at work.

New Lifestyle
D. B.

Being appreciative of the experiences that help me in life.

Beginning my adventures in the accomplishment of completion.

First, I have obtained my certification in floral design. Never have I been so overwhelmed.

So many times, I've wanted to complete a goal. And, there it is, all for me.

Always happy to help others, now, finally, I have completed a goal. I am successful!

If that's not a way to build self-confidence, what could be?

I so extol my teachers for their time and effort. They were encouraging my every move.

I think to myself, *A person needs some cheering along.*

Never will I forget the people who believed in me.

To the Women of The Gathering Place:
Sandina Tanguma

You inspire me every day.
We women have limitless strength.
We are beautiful, powerful and connected
to each other in more ways
than we can count. We are sisters

who support each other,
and we all have the potential
to shape our world into a better place—
to enact change and growth. I know
many of us are going through difficult times;

we struggle to survive. I am so thankful
that we have each other
and that we can have hope
and opportunity to change our lives.
I have lost hope before

and have felt like there was no way out
of despair. I know it is not easy
to get your life together and in a good place,
but I believe that we can and will
get through our struggles.

We all have the right
to pursue our dreams and to live
our lives to the fullest.

Homelessness in the Cold
Netta Tackwell

Homelessness in the winter is something one cannot comprehend fully until one has experienced it. There are many more individuals in our world who go day to day wondering how and where they are going to be able to find a place to be safe, warm and fed each night. Until one is out struggling to stay safe and wrapping themselves up in whatever they can find to stay warm, they can't appreciate the house they have to go to every day that has electricity, heat, food, a bed with blankets and pillows, a TV or radio for entertainment, or the safety that a house has.

Even though there are many shelters out there that say they will find a bed for you, this is not always true. One can spend their day going to or calling all the shelters to see if there is an opening, and, so many times, the answer is "no." Being homeless has effects on every aspect of our lives, and those who are fortunate enough to have a place of their own should maybe exchange places with a homeless person for a 24-hour period. Maybe, after doing so, more of those who are in a position to help in any way would start doing so, because nothing is a guarantee in life.

Not to Whine

Elizabeth Vonaarons

Sometimes it's easier to complain,
to whine
around the events in one's life.

I don't have any money,
I can't get the job I want,
I wish I had more time.

But whining doesn't solve anything
and it's self-destructive.
So get over it.

Write.
Yes, you can always write about it.
You can write a poem, short story or a play.

Maybe you can get someone to read that play,
or, better yet,
someone to perform the play.

Act it out.
Bring your characters to life.
It's a real kick to see your stories come to life.

Like in a film,
you write the story and it comes to life.
You can always write about it
as compared to whining about it.

Whining is self-destructive.
It does no good.
And it certainly doesn't make you happy.

Remember Me
BJ

When I cried, my tears fell silently in the night,
But then the sun came up, and you were there
With warm hugs and encouraging words to lift me up.
I walked away with hope that the day would get better.
Remember me, when you hug each other.

When I walked down the street, feeling invisible to people
Who wouldn't look at me, I knew I could come to you, that
You would see me as a human being, worthy of being seen.
I walked away with dignity, confident in my own self-worth.
Remember me, when you look at each other.

When I was hungry, you fed me, sitting down
To eat and share a conversation with me
That made my body and spirit feel full and whole again.
I walked away with energy to face my daily challenges.
Remember me, when you share meals and conversation together.

When I struggled with frustration, or anger boiling over,
You gave me the rules and boundaries with firm limits
To guide me toward self-control and cooperation.
I walked away with respect for myself and others.
Remember me, when you set limits with each other.

When I thought no one cared, or thought of me
As each year passed, marking my life upon this earth,
You celebrated my life with birthday parties.
I walked away knowing my life mattered.
Remember me, when you celebrate each other with birthday cake.

When I left this world, I left my footprints in your heart,
As you once placed your footprints in mine
When we shared our paths at The Gathering Place.
I walked away to peace and glory, leaving you behind to
Remember me, when you remember each other.

Remember me! Please, remember me!
Because we need each other to survive.
I gave you opportunities to love and care
While you gave me opportunities to thrive.
Remember me, because I'll be waiting for you on the other side.

Within These Walls

Joanna Saenz

Gathering Place
Spirits broken, wandering, wounded
looking for love and hope,
a safehouse
staff's warm smiles, embracing hugs
and non-judging hearts
embracing us
like a mother's womb and gentle touch.
Agape love comes from within these walls;
God holds my walls together,
tightly knit, exactly where he wanted
me to be at this moment.

Neither a Lender Nor a Borrower Be: Why?
Pepper-Lee

The vulnerability and purity
of the quite private circumstance
of being houseless
is actually quite the beauty.

The struggles and obstacles
form their way around
this experience as soon
as it touches the ground,
acting as fertilizer
for a fallen seed,
only to create a stronger
tree from that particular seed
almost immediately
after it has fallen down.

Many are called, yet few
are chosen. By far, is it only
kind of easy, yet we live
on a planet with no,
not one, yet many,
a component within the thing
that we live called humanity.

"Give to him who asks you,
and from him who wants to borrow
from you do not turn away."
The ground is deep; imagine that journey
to the earth's core.

The beginning.

Food Power
Sandina Tanguma

Food brings people together,
it connects them—think about it—
every culture in the world—
tortillas, pita bread, fry bread,
basmati rice, fried rice, Mexican rice,
custard, flan, crème brulee—
mmm, delicious….

The family meal, eating together, eating alone,
eating in a group, standing in line to get food, food bank,
food left on tables for people to take,
empty cupboards, full ones,
every little morsel a feast.
I watched teenage girls laughing at a homeless man searching
the trash for something to eat.
I watch people throwing food away like there's excess in the world,
like no one is hungry.

Conversation over a meal, preparing a meal,
tasting the love and care in a meal like spices and flavor.
Secret ingredients—what are mine?
How spicy am I? How sweet?
Do I provide nourishment? Do I share myself enough? Too much?
I'm hungry for a lot of things: I devour truth, sample beauty,
taste happiness and spoon in a generous helping
of life.

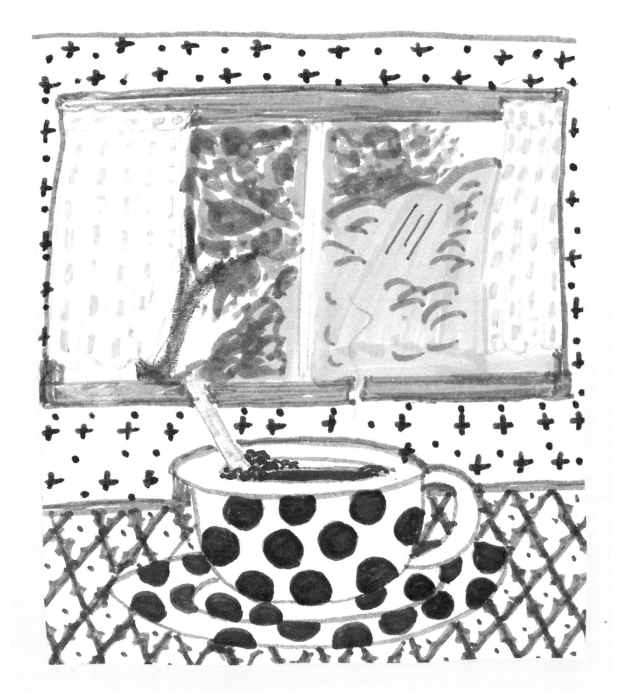

eb

How I Became Homeless
Jeanette R. Ambrose

My situation came about through no fault of my own. I rented an apartment; then, a week later it was bought by a new company. They did not want any of the previous tenants rented to by the former owners.

I had gone into the hospital for surgery and I had paid my rent, sent it in the mail from the hospital. When I came home I was told by the owners they did not receive the money.

I got the rent receipts and took them to the manager so he could copy them. The next day, I was told the manager was robbed. They stole $500 and my rent receipts.

So, consequently, I was evicted, even though I have the money order receipt numbers. At the time of the eviction, the money orders were not cashed. Without the actual receipt, I can't get my money back. So, $850 of my money is just sitting in limbo.

I feel like I am digging a hole and every time I throw out two shovels of dirt, someone up top is throwing one back in. And that's me, Jeanette—homeless, but not hopeless…

I have found help and hope at The Gathering Place. I got a permanent bed at The Delores Project and I am moving forward with my life.

Being homeless takes more strength and courage than the average person is aware of.

Being homeless is a state of body, not a state of mind.

Overnight in the Alley at 15 Degrees
Verna K. Nahulu

Nowhere to go…not wanting to trespass… I can do it…I'm tough!

I cleaned up a space, put my bags on the side, leaned back on the brown fence, put my knees up against my chest and prayed. "Lord, You know that I'm not tough without You. Keep me together with your warmth, because it's going to be a long night at 15 degrees."

Feeling strong and determined, I closed my eyes for a cold night's sleep. Out of nowhere came a voice, "Excuse me, lady. I brought you something. My mouth hung open, as out of his arms came a sleeping bag, a hot meal and a hot drink. He had come from the other side of the brown fence.

"Thank you so much!" I said. "Thank you!" He smiled and disappeared. I thought, "God, you work fast—thank you!" My eyes filled with tears of gratitude, as I slipped into the warm sleeping bag and munched on the food on the plate. I couldn't stop the tears. I let it come. Tears felt warm against my face. Before long, I lapsed into a warm sleep, and enjoyed the night.

I awoke the next morning surprised that the night had been warm in the sleeping bag. I looked around, embarrassed at my homelessness, but very warm. I remembered his face, my "fairy godfather."

Some time later, many days later, I sat at that spot—my good luck spot. Passing by with friends was a familiar face, saying, "Hi Verna!" I said, "Hi!" I stared at him.

"Oh, are you my fairy tale godfather?"

"Yes, Verna."

I immediately stood up, "Can I shake your hand?" I shook his hand and felt the hand of God. He smiled and we locked eyes, and slowly passed on. My eyes again poured warm tears down my face, which I was unable to wipe away. I will never forget his face, it's a permanence in my brain.

Thank you God. Thank you, thank you.

I haven't seen him again, but the brown fence is still there as a memorial to me. It's a memory forever to me, for many years to come.

I've since been in many homeless shelters, grateful for a roof over my head while I dream of having a home of my own one day. But the memory of my hero in this story will never be forgotten.

Winter
Risa

What is the cold?
It slaps me in the face
and taunts me to come

as I shiver and trudge
through the crisp snow,
looking for relief
to escape the frigid, frosty
and bitter cold.

It hurls me again,
blowing its volatile
wind against my frame.
I quiver,
it tackles me,

it threatens
my very life.

Journal
Paula Cordier

My best friend, I've neglected you
for so long. Always there for me,
listening to everything I have to say,
letting me cry, letting me laugh.
Never judging. Never spilling my secrets
or betraying me in any way.
You are the one I can always count on
when humans let me down.
You are the one who understands me
inside and out.

Words on paper.
The essence of my spirit and soul
in print.

Boarding School Dreams
BJ

Sometimes I dream we are holding hands
and walking down long hallways filled
with lonely, fresh-spent tears.
But, we don't cry; we have each other.

We look into each other's eyes and see
sweet secrets only little girls can share.

Laughter and dolls with tiny bead eyes
and rich black hair, carefully woven
from our mothers' heads.

Laughter and tiny acorn cups set
on a warm, flat stone in the sun
while we lounge in the shade.

Laughter beneath the piney bowers,
brown skin cooling with little sips
of water through smiling lips.

Sometimes when I dream, the hallways
echo with the lonely footsteps that
take us far away from our mothers,
but, we have each other and we hold hands.

I didn't know you then, of course,
I only see you now, sitting across from me,
crying the same tears, while your voice
repeats the echo of a childhood lost.
There were no dolls, no acorn cups,
no smiling lips, no laughter in the sun.

There is only you and me today,
touching each other's child
across a boarding school void.

Truth
Rita Gordon AKA Winston Salem

My worth is not determined by the price of my clothes, cost of my haircut, the car
    that I drive. Jeans and a t-shirt, wash and run hair, holes in my socks;
    I am acceptable, if only to me.
    Have any complaints? Speak to my maker; he made me alive.

My worth is not dependent on the love of a man,
    here today, gone tomorrow.
    It's my decision to live in peace or wallow in sorrow.
    Now it's peace, now it's sorrow—no condemnation left to borrow.

So my father neglected me, society rejects me
    as if I were invisible.
    People can choose to see whatever they want.
    Make a list; it won't make me not exist.
    Don't kick me out just because I'm a realist.

I am here; I am a force to be reckoned with.
    Don't like what you see? Turn away.
    Don't like what you hear? Cover your ears.
    Don't like what you read? Pull out your eyes.
    I am here to stay, come live or come may.

Truth isn't always welcome.
    I'm sorry if it makes you afraid.
    But truth is real; it lives, it breathes, it can be brutal or set you free.
    Look everywhere; it's you, it's me.

Truth won't go away.

    It won't be looked over, stepped over, trampled over, or lied over.

    Look again; it's there, it's giving you a glare,

    it's staring you in the eye, it will never say good-bye.

    Truth is a close cousin of mine, my best friend, my worst enemy, my ally.

Truth is in your shadow that walks with you at high noon; it's the heavy breathing

    in deepest sleep, it looks you in the mirror as you smile or weep.

    It's the <u>real</u> you, the <u>genuine</u> you, the <u>authentic</u> you,

    the you you're trying to kill pain from; it's yours to keep.

You may have trained it to go into hiding,

    covered it up with booze or drugs or cheap sex, or illusions of love pending,

    but its cute little eyes say, "Ha! You thought you could escape me?

    Silly person, you can't flee truth," it says with a snarl in its teeth.

Maybe you can try. Go ahead, try! Kill it, steal it, flirt with it, cheat on it,

    fuck it! You can't flee truth you silly goose.

    What did you think? This isn't Mother Goose!

Truth is like water flowing through your hands;

    until you accept it, it eludes you.

    Hit your head! Get a concussion!

    Wake up, man! This is your life,

    not a delusion!

As seen by
Rita Gordon AKA Winston Salem

Empty
eb

Empty empty
shot through space
going—shooting
shooting shooting
        past this star
and solar
        system into the next,
one layer to the next to
another…

The opposite of full,
only result of this journey is to
another destination.
When you arrive, you look back
and say
        how did I get here?

Where did I
take a wrong
turn
        and
allow someone
to bring me
here?

When was I vulnerable too
much,
gave too much and asked
        for so little in return?
Or is what I asked for too
little?
        Is it even?

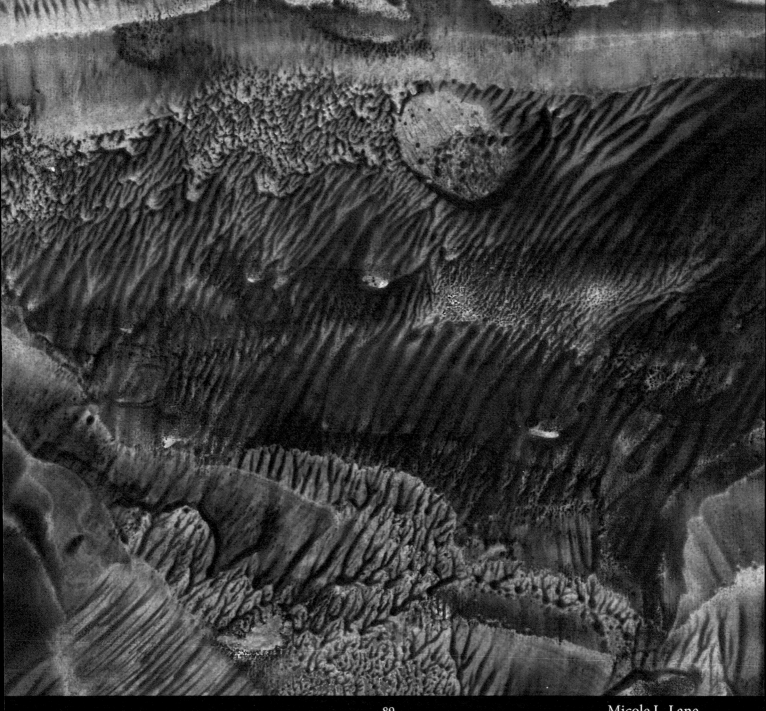

Micole L. Lane

ADVICE
Kay L. Eshelman

The best advice I can give to those in the situation of too much month, and not enough funds is:

Hang out with others.
Work hard.
Get schooling.
Ask for help.
Never, never sleep in the street or a park, especially if you carry identification.
Try to get good references.
Some help agencies destroy any plan to have life, liberty and the pursuit of happiness.
Be prepared to exit any facility, which may only give you a few minutes to leave, after any lame
        excuse. Look for the exit signs.
If you work hard at it, you can stop criminals from grabbing the credit you have.

Too often, "bad guys" win.
Pay your rent.
Pay your bills.
Get credit.
While you are renting, if you spot trouble coming up:
Pay your rent in advance.
Give notice.
Always pay your bills.

To keep healthy:
Work out at the YMCA. [Health insurance may be lower if you join a YMCA Program.]

Some "musts" to prevent homelessness:
Find a job, any job!
Make sure your credit is good.
Establish a help line of people who can help and really care.

Remember!
God and the world are watching.
No bad can come to you if you pray and are prepared for whatever may come up.
Shelter is a legal right.

Broken

C.M. Davidson-Sole

She sits in the weeds
and she ponders; she looks
around, her mind wanders.

She appears to be worn,
so lifeless, forlorn;
in her eyes you can tell
she's exhausted.

Her confidence has been
broken; you can tell
by her words, unspoken.

She sits on her perch
and you know she's been hurt,
because she's silent,

and keeps to herself.

Government Words
Kim Holder

"Homeless?"
    No. Without a place to live.
"Housing? Shelter?"
    No. I have a home. I live in a dormitory.

When you say it that way,
I lose my song.
I lose my voice
and my soul.

It's much the same with all the words
you make up, Mr. and Mrs. Government.
I can't tell you how many times I hate
my home to be called a "unit."

It's much like what you did
to the original inhabitants
here in the States and Canada.

"Indians."
    No. Cherokee. Apache. Hopi.
    Nations.

1. Do you want a song?

2. Do you have a soul?

3. Live it then!

Mother
Rogene Munnell

She expressed courage every day.

Didn't take "no guff off no man;"
Shut a window just in time to avoid an attacker trying to get in;
Jumped off a bus to break up a girl fight; she believed in fair play.

She listened to God's voice to keep herself safe;
Was kind, sympathetic, enthusiastic, musical, enjoyed simple things;
She was a reflection of a strong "Mother God."

She shared her pain and I endured and carried it.
Along with her courage, intuition and empathy.
She was a philosopher and so am I… a philosopher with a good ear.

LOOK AT ME!
Brenda Joyce Haynesworth

When I walk down the street
They turn their faces,
They look away,
At the ground they rather see.
I talk rather loud cuz
I NEED THEM TO
LOOK AT ME!

When I enter a room,
They exit the place,
They move to another location,
Out the door they go!
I smell really bad, no place to get clean,
I NEED THEM TO
LOOK AT ME!

When I stand by the road,
They ignore my sign,
They speed up to pass,
Rolling up their windows fast!
I beg out of desire for a deeper cause,
I NEED THEM TO
LOOK AT ME!

When I dress in my street best,
They shake their heads,
They put up "the hand"
To prevent me from getting close!
I put on my clothes to hide my shame,
I NEED THEM TO
LOOK AT ME!

When I raise my fist and yell at myself,
They fear my ranting,
They disregard my humanity,
Making a clean getaway to the
Other side of the street!
I'm insane from their neglect
And standards of right,
I NEED THEM TO
LOOK AT ME!

When I go home at night and
Fall asleep in my box,
They don't see the hurt,
They don't see the guilt!
I'm a closet genius in rags and riches,
I NEED THEM TO
LOOK AT ME!

When I get up the next morning
And start over again,
They have different faces,
They drive different cars;
I see them as the same old crowd,
I NEED THEM TO
LOOK AT ME!

eb

Destination Unknown
Leticia D. Tanguma

Where do I go now?
I've eaten,
I've slept,

I've taken care of
my basic human needs
at shelters;
I have no money,
no nice clothes.
I do have dignity, however.

So, where do I dance,
where do I sing,
where do I write and draw,
where do I dream?

It's cold,
it's cold out there,
judging eyes,
dangerous hands.
I'm not paranoid.

My loved ones and I
have been raped,
have been beaten with bats,
have been choked,
have been spat at.

I will find a place, for, after all,
I do have dignity.
This has nothing to do
with self-esteem, or the lack thereof;
I did not ask this upon myself,
"ask for it."

I do dance
and sing
and write
and draw
and dream.

Bedouin

Kim Holder

Homeless one, don't
despair,
you are free

of house, bill and rule.
You are a gypsy
now and can go

far and wide,
no yoke around
your neck.

      Rejoice!

First months
are boot camp,
walking

for hours
all day and night,
carrying

all you own.
After 10 weeks,
you'll sail, see all

there is
to see and be truly

      a wandering spirit.

Still Reeling from Homelessness

eb

It is so nice now to wake up in a place that is all my own, with gleaming floors and the sun shining in. There is no noise. No one is barking at you to wake up and get going. Even as I enjoy my beautiful little cottage with working hot water, a stove, my own bathroom, etc. I can't believe this is me. Every morning I feel like a princess. Thanks to God's mercy and a Section 8 Lottery, I was able to move into this place. God knows I would not last long without a place. The habits that bring homelessness are still there: struggling to pay bills; lack of belief in myself; wanting to help people. Some people take advantage of this when they see it in you. I am learning the lesson to "think of myself first."

I love my tiny new home. But, flashbacks to the time when in winter I had no place to go, remain. How lucky I was that a friend came along when I was going to sleep in my "illegal" truck. Friends say, "You would have froze."

Always, I think back and remind myself of all that I have been through. Women especially, have it harder. All of the hygiene we have to take care of makes it harder for us. People who have mates to help, maybe are luckier. But sometimes this person may push you to the limits and doesn't understand. Men are stronger, and don't require the extra rest that women do, at that "time of the month."

I keep thinking of the things I should have done, could have done, or should not have done. But, I remain thankful for the small piece of Heaven I have in my home, every day.

Time
Sandina Tanguma

I think of it like a liquid.
You can try to cup it in your palms,
it trickles through the spaces,
then escapes,
falls back to earth.
Sometimes you want to hold to yourself,
to hoard, store excess,
lock away for future use,
yet it is always spreading boundlessly
outward,
beyond capture or pause,
ticking,
and, once it's here, it's gone.
That moment you need,
you yearn for,
brought up in memory,
evidence of its passing everywhere,
marked in
weathered buildings,
faded photographs,
and your own soul, keeping it—
a marker,
chapter:
time.

Lost In Siberia
Kim Holder

After four days
of blizzards, voices
     and hallucinations,

walking alone

down Jefferson Davis Highway,
   freezing cold at a truck stop,

no check for three months,
   on this journey from Utah
         to Virginia.

I warm up
     in the ladies room
for ten minutes. The moon

is almost full.
        I just passed

a frozen-dead sparrow
standing still on the earth
     with snow on it.

That could happen to me.

I spot food
on the icy, dirty, oily
    driveway.

A hot dog.

I pick it up
    and bite.
It's frozen.

I think of
Ivan Denisovich.

in the Siberian
labor camps.

I am there.

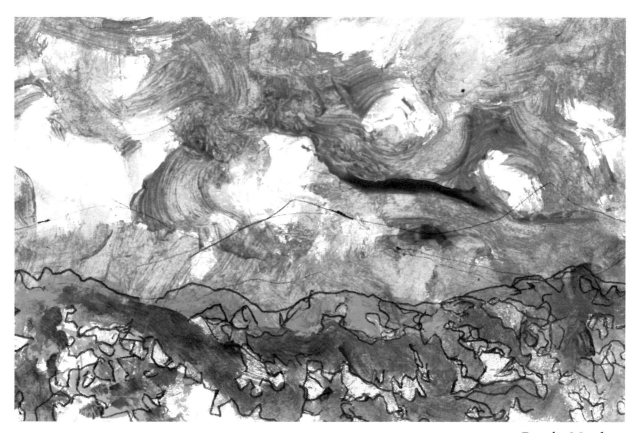

Brooke Meadow

Dear Friend

Leticia D. Tanguma

Thank you for being
a presence of dignity.
When you speak to people,
when you write,
when you draw,
you recognize us,
even when we are covered
in the street's dust, you recognize us.
You recognize us.

The Whisper of the Wind
Peg Butler

The courage to feel
the mystery of a gentle hug
from a person you love
is like the whisper of the wind
that stirs up love,
that kisses your cheek
and dances at your feet.

The four seasons are a mystery
to us—winter, with the courage
to go out in the cold, spring,
with the whisper of the wind,
summer, hugging us in warm
sunlight, and fall, the call
of short daylight.

I walk the streets homeless,
with a home with no walls.
I have the courage to find a spot
to rest my head,
with no pillow for my bed.
The whisper of the wind
surrounds me
and the mystery
of how I got here
profounds me.

There are no hugs
of encouragement, just
diligence to walk
in a place with no windows
and doors to lock
and keep me safe.

Life is a process, not an event,
and my process takes courage,
one day, one night
at a time.

Homelessness
Paula Cordier

The chilly winter wind cuts across my face as my fingers grow numb in my thin gloves. I'm sitting at a bus stop and it's night out. I stomp my feet, hoping to bring at least a flicker of warmth to them. Cars are whizzing past me, and I feel invisible.

A lump starts growing in my throat, getting bigger, until I'm unable to swallow. Scalding hot tears burn my face, carried away by the cold. The people in the cars don't see me.

My mind gets carried away thinking of them, probably going home from work. Home to families or people that care about them as I sit at the bus stop alone.

I have no spot in this world to call my own. I feel such a deep loneliness that permeates my whole soul. There's a deep longing to be in one of those cars that are speeding past. A longing to be warm, on my way to a home with colorful, cheery curtains, in a cozy kitchen with a family that awaits.

The bus pulls up, harsh brakes bring me out of my reveries. I climb on, not knowing where I'm going.

Sharon Kumm

The Group
Elizabeth Vonaarons

Inspiration,
Eclectic personalities,
Buggy pushing,
Yes, all of the above.

We are all unique.
Our spirit of life prevails.
Far from being alone,
We can share

Our joy,
Our challenges,
Our passion,
For it is our passion that guides us.

No matter what,
No matter how,
We strive to be
Human,

To care,
To love,
To accept
Others

For who they are,
For what they believe,
For what they see as their
Destiny.

We come together,
Strong as one,
In harmony,
Our journey come to be

A place of refuge,
A place to think,
A place to be
Whoever we choose to be.

The group connects
The spirit of hope,
The advent of joy
For all beings in life to see.

What I Learned in a Shelter
C.M. Davidson-Sole

Fighting, backbiting, name calling, and brawling, everyday social unrest.
It's like watching preschoolers who have a conniption over places, stuff and a bed.

Mine! Mine! Mine! Goes the cadence of voices from tired people, upset.
People are pushing and shoving to be first in line just to get a decent night's rest.

Yet, among all the brawling, bitching and whining, some people are never upset.
They just roll with the punches and sit on their haunches, and seem to take life in their stride.
They just take it all in, and still manage to grin, and take the day as GOD gives it to them.

The human race is a funny thing, especially when we are under stress.
Some people are calm as they journey along, and some people are just a big mess.

Winter
Maria Rita Figueiredo Wano

Lessons of a single year
succeed for decades,
centuries and millennia.

Seasonal winters precede the springtime.
The anticipation of both are predictable.
Unpredictable are the spiritual winters,
and we are often unprepared for them.
We lack reserves of warmth, of protection,
and we are exposed
to the intemperateness of nature.

Have I been a grasshopper who did not
anticipate the cold days?

Or, did I just try to grasp the meaning—
so subtle and difficult to define.
Unconditional love, the living
and experiencing this kind of love,
could certainly lead to the security
of living under a roof, away
from the windy storms and crude nature.

Did I really offer unconditional love?

BJ

Day by Day
Delores Angele Woodruff

Day by day, as I walk the street,
I'm careful not to miss a beat.
Day by day, I open my eyes;
sometimes, I sit and cry.
Day by day, I stand in the rain;
my heart begins to feel the pain.

Day by day, I begin to think
of all without anything to drink,
not a roof overhead to warm the soul,
being outside in the cold,

how blessed we are to stand in this rain,
and go back in without feeling the pain.

Breathing
Sharon Kumm

Breathing, deeply, feeling that
pain in my side saying I wonder
if it wants to be friends again.
Something in me wants to be there.
If I hadn't written about what was
so important to me, maybe I would
have kept what was working. Sky
deep the distance between them.
Maybe I was learning to climb in
again, not like darkness exactly,
since the sky is its twin, neither
one definable in the interim
called entering,
one step, the child in pain saying
thank you. For the grownup,
everything spanned feeling.

Rain

Micole L. Lane

Rain down and read
the colors of my heart, and feel
the seed that I am, I will be.
And, if you do not want me
to be, I will get up and say,

I am the realness to the feelness,
the color I see in your face
is the sweetness of red
and blue. Your face can see
chaos with the days of sadness
in the time of sorrow.

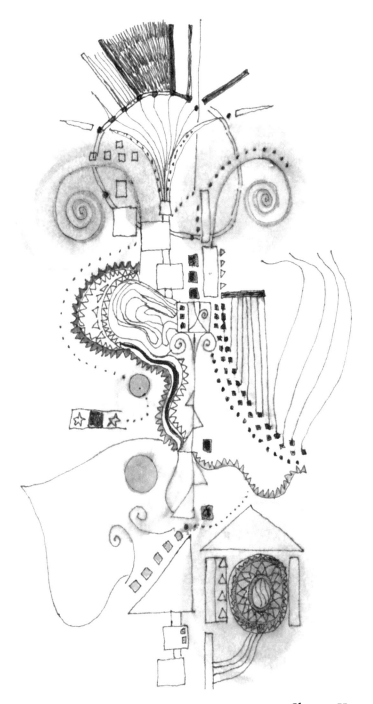

Sharon Kumm

Memorial Wall
BJ

When I first saw the memorial plaques on the garden wall of our old building, I was surprised that, even in death, we are remembered by The Gathering Place. But then I thought, why not, when the staff, volunteers, funders and other supporters have made caring about us and uplifting our lives their priority.

I read the names of these women and marvel that their lives are not that different from my own, with all the struggles, heartaches, and even joy that comes with being homeless, impoverished or just down and out in spirit and mind. And I use the word "joy" because it is a strong word, beyond happiness, and we are strong women who can endure the difficult challenges that come with poverty and homelessness. There is joy in our relationships with each other, in our sharing of resources, education and information that is relevant to our lives, in coming to The Gathering Place and being greeted by our names, and in being known for who we really are and not for who you might assume we are. The joy is there, even if we don't recognize it for what it is, because we are too busy and involved with trying to make it through one more day, and then another.

Like so many others, I used to feel forgotten and alone until I came to The Gathering Place. I used to worry that I would die feeling unknown, a whisper on the earth that no one could hear. The memorial plaques on the garden wall gave me hope that that would not happen. But, just to be sure, I began my own campaign to be included on the wall, asking a couple of friends and advocates to remember to put me there when I walk away, no matter where I am when it's my turn to leave this earth. In fact, when it's my turn, I hope my plaque says "BJ was here!"

Put This in Your Book!!
Brenda Joyce Haynesworth

Put this in your book!
Tell them I'm soaring with the eagles;
Tell them I'm eating the grapes of joy;
Tell them I'm pushing the limits of my abilities,
And have broken free from the deep despair that was holding me down!

Put this in your book!
Tell them to look at the beauty inside;
Tell them to stretch their wings and fly;
Tell them to take a leap of faith,
And find the sweet release from the freedom of a self-propelling life!

Put this in your book!
Tell them to stop listening to the naysayer;
Tell them to pick their own brains;
Tell them they have all the right answers flowing within,
And to value their own self-importance by being confident and smart!

Put this in your book!
Tell them to never give up in this fight to survive;
Tell them to pick their battle;
Tell them they are significant to our community,
And that all things are possible if they appreciate the resources given!

Put this in your book!
Tell them they are Powerful beyond measure;
Tell them they are Precious to our society;
Tell them they are Prepared to meet the challenges of life,
And they too can soar with eagles, eat grapes of joy, and push the limits of their abilities!

Put this in your book so all who read will know…

Thank You
Sandina Tanguma

I do not know your name
but
thank you for being strong,
for having a smile on your face
though breaking inside.
Thank you for expecting a smile in return.
Those connections, those kind words—
they've mattered.

I've seen we are all caught in a flood;
thank you for reaching out, for not only
wanting us all to stay afloat, but
for us to get out of the water.

Thanks for showing your dignity,
your grace, your love.
Thank you for telling
your story—and knowing
that it deserves to be told.

Thanks for all those good times
we've had—laughing, being mischievous,
gossiping—just being the beautiful
women that we are.

For hearing my dreams, my struggles,
and allowing me to hear yours.
Thank you.

About the Authors

There are many stereotypes about people who are homeless or experiencing poverty. Yet like any other group, there is great individual variety in background and levels of achievement, some of which belies what we think we know to be true.

Of the writers included in this publication, nearly half represent a racial minority. They range in age from women in their 20's to senior citizens beyond the age of 70. About two-thirds are between the ages of 40 and 60.

The writers are generally well educated, with levels ranging from 11th grade to people with master's degrees. In fact 33 percent have a bachelor's or master's degree and an additional 12 percent have an associate degree. Over one-fourth of the writers are currently enrolled in college, are in temporary or part-time jobs, or attend a job training program.

The biographies below offer a more personal insight into the lives of the writers.

BJ is a Sicangu Lakota of the Great Teton Nation of Peoples. A victim, along with her people, of abusive practices used by the government to "civilize" them, she found her voice through healing poetry written during therapy, which helped free her from the old shame and anger that once held her captive. The Gathering Place has provided a safe community in which she can express herself and share her journey with others, through writing and talking. She walks a healing path and invites her readers to walk with her.

Brenda Joyce Haynesworth has written extensively of her spiritual thoughts, beliefs, and life experiences. She is contemplating what to do with the next decade as she approaches her 60th birthday, anticipating that these will be the best ten years of her life. She has applied for admission to a graduate program in Leadership and Organization in preparation for this new phase, hoping to receive training in guiding churches toward their best practices while addressing the problems presented by the world today. She is the proud mother of three adult daughters.

Brooke Meadow writes to express her thoughts and feelings. She finds the process cathartic, but also wants to inspire people to think. The Gathering Place provides her with a sense of community. She likes sharing meals with the other women and enjoys the collaboration and feedback of creative arts workshops like Writers' Group and The Card Project. Now that her daughter is grown, her greatest challenge has been adjusting to living alone. Her hope for the future is for world peace.

Delores Angele Woodruff writes because it gives her inner strength and a heart "vibe" like no other; it sets her free. She appreciates that The Gathering Place offers people in difficult circumstances a place to get out of the cold, establish connections with others, and share a hot meal. Despite the challenge of managing her mental health issues, she is happy. Delores hopes to publish some of her short stories and a book about bipolar disorder. She describes herself as having, "the biggest, most beautiful heart in the world."

eb has discovered through writing the patterns that bring people to homelessness, a journey she records as a form of therapy. She finds great support through interacting with kindred spirits who are struggling and having experiences similar to her own. Proud of her past and of the family from which she came, eb hopes to return to them some day. She understands that many women get caught up in lives they didn't choose and knows it is a feat to get free of that life; she feels she is in the final stages of that effort.

Elizabeth Vonaarons writes because it helps her be who she wants to be, as it takes her into a world of make believe and of truth, allowing free expression while creating something of meaning. She very much enjoys everything life has to offer, gaining inspiration from other writers in Writers' Group, and hopes to get more of her writing published, a play produced or a screenplay made into a movie. For Elizabeth, The Gathering Place allows people to share and feel comfort and joy. She has no regrets about the past and looks forward to the future.

Essie Mae Thomas writes because she sees this skill as a gift given by God. She's in the process of writing a book, hoping it will be published and possibly made into a movie some day. Reaching people and sharing her testimonies to bring them hope and happiness is a top priority for Essie. She lives out her philosophy of contentment each day, knowing the sky is the limit if you believe in your dreams. It is her aim to be content with the blessings God has given her.

Jennie K. Foster aspires to become a successful writer, but for now she gains great satisfaction from knowing she has completed a major writing project, a children's story. Being kind and loving to all is a top priority for Jennie, a woman who strives to find a positive message in everything she does. She finds that The Gathering Place is a community that gives unconditionally to under-represented women while asking for nothing in return.

Joanna Saenz writes because it provides her a form of expression and a sense of freedom. As a single mother managing the demands of two young boys, she values the support system provided by The Gathering Place to her family. By helping and inspiring others who want to better themselves, she hopes to repay humanity for all the gifts she has received. She lives every day to the fullest and chooses not to feel defeated. She finds happiness in her children and her relationship with her Creator. If she could sum up herself and her family in a word, it would be love.

Kathy Lakes was among the first women in the Writers' Group to express an interest in writing a book that would bring a broader understanding of how women experience homelessness. She finds that writing her thoughts and ideas give her insight into herself. At The Gathering Place, Kathy has met many people—through The Card Project, knitting, and crochet classes—and has learned from each of them. At some time in the future, she would like to sell some of her writing or the things she makes. She wants the world to know that she is proud of her husband, Tim.

Kim Holder, a writer and a poet, has struggled with mental illness for 28 years. Homeless for seven of those years, she traveled all over the world, once finding herself living on the streets of Paris. Writing offers Kim an opportunity for self-expression, creativity, and the chance to both educate and inform others. She describes The Gathering Place as a warm, safe, and friendly escape for the neglected and bewildered. The single parent of a grown son, she now finds love and comfort with her cat, Rosie. Kim hopes to live in peace and leave the world a better place.

Leticia D. Tanguma is a writer and an artist who loves to tell stories through writing. After she was laid off from work, she went back to school to pursue a degree in what she most loves—creative writing. Her genres include first person experiences, current and historical events, fiction, and magical realism. Her ultimate writing goal is to add understanding, critique, and even humor to our human connections, and to use her writing as a bridge to making these connections possible among a variety of people.

Maria Rita Figueiredo Wano was born and educated in Brazil but has lived in the United States for many years. Her writing, in both English and Portuguese, about everyday experiences has been helpful to her when dealing with the stresses of her life. She is visually impaired at present and is waiting for surgery to deal with cataracts and macular degeneration. Maria has found support and community at The Gathering Place. She is proud of her family and friendships and of the fact that she very recently became an American citizen.

Netta Tackwell writes to share what she feels and thinks and lets her knowledge, feelings, and experiences come out in the open. Despite the fact that she has lived with abuse throughout her life, and dealt with serious medical problems, she attended nursing school and had the opportunity to work with patients with many complex medical situations. She was able to see success with her patients and she can coax a smile or a laugh from the most difficult cases. She is hoping for safe, stable, clean housing in the near future and the opportunity to write a book about her life.

Peg Butler is both a writer and a poet. She likes The Gathering Place because it not only helps women with all kinds of needs but also provides an opportunity to meet and talk with women about things that are challenging to them. She writes to express herself, to describe how she sees other people and situations, and to help others through her words. Peg hopes to continue writing on a regular basis and to perhaps see her writing in other books.

Risa finds that writing gives her clarity, helping to identify what she is thinking and feeling. The Gathering Place provides her with the opportunity to reconnect with old friends and meet new ones while deriving great happiness from seeing people's lives changed. Her greatest challenge is to continue pursuing her dreams no matter what the obstacles may be, hoping to become a teacher, an evangelist, and an artist. She is proud of her family—her mother, who always believed in families, her husband for never giving up, and her children, who have faced difficulties and met challenges.

Rita Gordon AKA Winston Salem writes short stories and poetry, finding that writing helps to clarify the "jumbled-up" thoughts in her head. As a participant in both Writers' Group and The Card Project, she appreciates the recognition she has received for her writing, hoping to have it published one day. Her greatest struggles have been to establish financial stability and overcome her lifelong shyness and low self-esteem. By writing of her experiences of racism and prejudice, she hopes to help people who are facing the same issues.

Sandina Tanguma is a writer and artist for whom creativity provides healing, helping her through difficult times. She feels a great sense of accomplishment and pride when she writes, knowing she has told a part of her own greater story while encouraging others to add something beautiful to the world through their own writing. A senior at The University of Colorado Denver majoring in theater, film, and television, she plans to use her degree to work in both areas, while also publishing novels and collections of short stories, and traveling the world.

VAL writes because she wants to share how she sees the world around her. She appreciates the differences of people and their encounters on this planet. And, although there have been surprises—positive and negative—she is satisfied with what she has shared and learned through the years. In her first encounter with The Gathering Place, she was pleased to see that everyone was treated with equal respect, creating a sense of family in this community. She still feels that way each time she walks in the door. VAL enjoys living in the moment, in all its simplicity, while her hope for the future is to accept change without fear.

Verna K. Nahulu writes because she feels she must. Words rush around in her heart and mind, "like dictation from the angels, and they have a lot to say," she reports. Sometimes, as her pen touches paper, Verna's soul smiles and then the fun begins—happiness grabs her and she feels alive. The Gathering Place nourishes her heart and soul, providing the impetus to carry on, no matter what. She is happiest when she lets go and "allows God to write it down." Being a Hawaiian Kahuna healer helps her to "hug life itself" for the goodness of it all.

Authors

Artwork in *One Day, One Night at a Time*
is by women in the Writers' Group.
The cover art is by Sharon Kumm.

Artists

BJ	21, 83, 109
Brooke Meadow	29, 101
eb	79, 95
Kay L. Eshelman	59
Leticia D. Tanguma	3, 39
Micole L. Lane	9, 89
Risa	33, 71
Sharon Kumm	13, 51, 105, 113
VAL	44, 63

The Denver Shelter System and The Gathering Place

In 1986, when The Gathering Place was founded, we estimated that on any given night there were about 2,500 people who were homeless. Women and children were just beginning to be visible in the population and might have comprised about 10%. Most services were run by religious institutions and were designed to meet the needs of homeless men. Specifically, men slept on cots in churches and in emergency shelters. The existing shelters closed during the day so that the men would have to go out, find jobs, and begin to put their lives together.

As women became more prevalent in the homeless population, many shelters responded as best they could; first, finding unexpected corners and places in their facilities for women and families, and then ultimately developing a few shelters that offered specific services for women or families and a modicum of privacy. Still, overnight shelters required everyone to leave for the day, which created a challenging and unsafe situation for women. Faced with spending their days walking the streets, often with children in hand, the experience of being out for the day was entirely different for women than it was for men. Due to this reality, The Gathering Place was started to offer women and children a safe place to go during the day, and a place where they could use their days productively rather than losing their time to street survival. In a small storefront on Santa Fe Drive, the initial philosophy of The Gathering Place was to offer hospitality – a safe place, food to eat, telephones, resources, friends, and a community of support. Within a short time, the storefront became too crowded and the service needs grew. In 1990, The Gathering Place moved to our current location at 1535 High Street.

Women, children, and families have been the largest growing segment of the homeless population since that time. A 2012 study found that on any given night in Denver there are approximately 12,000 people who are homeless. Of those, 44% are women and 64% are people in families. For the first time, people who are transgendered were included in the count. The programs and services of The Gathering Place remain more in need than ever.

Over the years, the philosophy of The Gathering Place has remained essentially unchanged. We have expanded our organization to serve women, children, and people who are transgendered, who are either homeless or those who are housed and experiencing poverty. We believe in the power of community and that hope is a force for change. We are willing to hold that hope for others when they are unable to hold it for themselves. We know that essential resources are paramount to moving forward in life and we understand that when times are the most challenging, it is personal relationships that get us through: the knowledge that someone else believes in you when you don't believe in yourself; the thoughtfulness that comes from sharing and understanding the value of a multitude of perspectives.

The Gathering Place offers an unparalleled set of resources from which each person can choose what she needs in her life. And, The Gathering Place offers unconditional acceptance and support no matter what decisions a person is making now or has made in the past. We believe that everyone is good and valuable just as she is today and every person is deserving of hope, love, dignity, and respect.

Index

Access Housing

Access Housing helps homeless families regain their independence primarily by preventing homelessness. In addition to short-term emergency shelter, this organization provides case management and financial assistance for housing, medical care, education, utilities, and transportation expenses. They also offer education and life skills training.

DenUM

Denver Urban Ministries is a nonprofit crisis center. They offer employment-related individual counseling and case management, food through a choice model food pantry, and support services, such as access to computers, transportation, resume assistance, and, as funds are available, assistance with rent and utilities.

Safehouse Denver

Safehouse Denver provides emergency shelter to women and families who are escaping domestic violence. Safehouse also provides off-site counseling and resources for women who are not in shelter and facing issues of violence.

Section 8

The Section 8 voucher program is a federal program for rental assistance for individuals and families who are below 50% of the area median income. In 2012, a single person in Denver had to make less than $27,250 to qualify for Section 8; a family of 2 had to make less than $31,150. The program is funded by Housing and Urban Development (HUD) and administered locally by the Denver Housing Authority (DHA). Twice each year, DHA holds a lottery to determine who gets vouchers.

Senior Resource Center

Although often called the "Senior Resource Center," the organization that serves seniors in Denver who are homeless is actually "Senior Support Services." This organization offers day shelter, coffee, a hot meal a day, and case management services for seniors who are homeless. In addition, they assist with accessing public benefits and housing.

SSDI/SSI

SSDI is Social Security Disability Income and SSI is Supplemental Security Income. These two public benefit programs offer monthly financial payments to qualifying disabled people. The process to obtain either SSDI or SSI often takes years.

The Aristocrat

The Aristocrat is a motel run by the Volunteers of America where unaccompanied women or families can stay for up to 12 days while they find more permanent shelter.

The Brandon Center

The Brandon Center is a shelter run by the Volunteers of America for women and families who are homeless or experiencing domestic violence. People can stay for up to 90 days and receive services to help them gain housing.

The Delores Project

The Delores Project is a 50-bed shelter for women who are unaccompanied, meaning they do not have children with them. The majority of the beds are transitional where women receive services to help them move into more permanent housing. A few beds are reserved for women in an emergency situation.

Theodora House

Theodora House is a 25-bed shelter run by the Volunteers of America for women who are unaccompanied.

Founded in 1986, The Gathering Place is a nonprofit organization in Denver, Colorado that has been a leader in serving women, children, and people who are transgendered, and experiencing homelessness and poverty. Offering an impressive array of programs and services, The Gathering Place has a unique philosophy that focuses on building positive relationships and offering choice to its members. In a community of safety and acceptance, The Gathering Place believes in hope as an important change agent and that the power of community can transform lives.

For more information or to make a donation to The Gathering Place, please visit our website at www.tgpdenver.org.

1535 High Street, Denver CO 80218

The Gathering Place®
a refuge for rebuilding lives

CPSIA information can be obtained
at www.ICGtesting.com
Printed in the USA
BVIC012340230513
321483BV00001B

* 9 7 8 1 9 3 7 8 6 2 3 8 1 *